My Favorite Failure

My Favorite Failure

How Setbacks Can Lead to Learning and Growth

Ronald A. Beghetto
Laura McBain

ROWMAN & LITTLEFIELD
Lanham • Boulder • New York • London

Published by Rowman & Littlefield
An imprint of The Rowman & Littlefield Publishing Group, Inc.
4501 Forbes Boulevard, Suite 200, Lanham, Maryland 20706
www.rowman.com

86-90 Paul Street, London EC2A 4NE, United Kingdom

British Library Cataloguing in Publication Information Available

Library of Congress Cataloging-in-Publication Data

Names: Beghetto, Ronald A., 1969– author. | McBain, Laura, 1974– author.
Title: My favorite failure : how setbacks can lead to learning and growth / Ronald A. Beghetto, Laura McBain.
Description: Lanham : Rowman & Littlefield, [2022] | Includes bibliographical references. | Summary: "The stories we included in this book help to highlight the nuances, colors, and textures of failure"—Provided by publisher.
Identifiers: LCCN 2021055279 (print) | LCCN 2021055280 (ebook) | ISBN 9781475856569 (cloth) | ISBN 9781475856576 (paperback) | ISBN 9781475856583 (epub)
Subjects: LCSH: Academic achievement. | Failure (Psychology)
Classification: LCC LB1062.6 .B455 2022 (print) | LCC LB1062.6 (ebook) | DDC 371.2/8—dc23/eng/20211230
LC record available at https://lccn.loc.gov/2021055279
LC ebook record available at https://lccn.loc.gov/2021055280

To my daughter, Olivia, may you always carry confidence, hope, and joy even in the darkest moments of the setbacks you encounter in learning and life.

—Ronald A. Beghetto

To my mother, whose love has always supported me through my successes and failures.

—Laura McBain

Contents

Preface   ix

Acknowledgments   xi

Introduction   1

1   Expectation   11

2   Frozen   19

3   Curiosity   27

4   Disappointment   35

5   Perspective   47

6   Guilt   55

7   Surprise   63

8   Embarrassment   71

9   Honesty   79

10   Humility   89

Epilogue   95

References   101

About the Authors   105

Preface

In education and in design there is a lot of talk about failure. We have taglines like "fail forward," "fail early and often," "learn from your mistakes," "lean into failure," "have grit," and even "let's have a bias toward failure." However, despite these well-intended phrases, we believe there is still more to understand about what it means to experience failure and learn from those experiences, even (and maybe especially) when those failures are painful.

What would it mean if we could collect and share stories of failures with our students, children, and colleagues? Would it help us get beyond the empty platitudes and, instead, help us consider the often messy, emotional journey of what it means to fail in and out of school? Would such stories of everyday failure help us better understand not only the journey of education and learning, but also the journey of the human experience?

We went on a quest to better understand the fabric of failure—the feelings, the principles, the tenets, and tentacles of failure that stick with us even after the moment of failure has long since receded in our memories. This book is an attempt to see the facets of failure through the lens of everyday experiences of those willing to take the beautiful risk of sharing their stories.

Our hope is that you will not just read these stories but share them with colleagues and young people. More than that we also hope that these stories will prompt you to share your own favorite failures with others to establish learning and life situations where people are willing to take beautiful risks, express their full humanity, and support each other in the learning that comes from our inevitable setbacks, stumbles, and failures along the way.

Acknowledgments

This book would not be possible without the fearless storytellers who opened their hearts and turned their moments of failure into stories we can all learn from.

We collected dozens of stories. Some of those stories are featured in this book, including stories from: Elyse Burden; Garrett J. Jaeger, PhD; Mihyun Han, PhD; Sophia McGovern; Charmaine Mercer; Punya Mishra; Michael J. Pryor; Wendy Ross; Kami Thordarson; Shagun Singha; Sae Saem Yoon; and Mariia Vitrukh. Although we were not able to include all the stories we received, we appreciate the beautiful risks taken by everyone who is willing to share stories of favorite failures with others. We hope that they and everyone who reads this book will continue to share their stories with others.

The cover image was designed by Cynthia Zhou and iterated on by the design team, Kathi Ha, at Rowman & Littlefield.

We want to also thank Tom Koerner, vice president/publisher for Education at Rowman & Littlefield, for his encouragement and assistance with this project as well as Carlie Wall and Catherine Herman for the editorial support on this book.

Last, but certainly not least, we are grateful to our community of colleagues, friends, and family for the support, thinking, and inspiration they provided while we developed this book.

Introduction

WHY THIS BOOK?

This project started through our own conversations and stories about educational setbacks and our work trying to support young people and educators in establishing learning environments supportive of creative risk-taking (Beghetto, 2019) and deep learning (Kapur, 2008, 2016), which inevitably involves setbacks and failures (von Theinen, Meinel, & Corazza, 2017). We realized that we, much like many educators, didn't spend a lot of time talking about or sharing failures with our students and colleagues. Sure, we were aware (sometimes painfully aware) of our own prior failures. However, when we did share and invite stories of failures, it served as a bridge between setback and new learning.

Even though there is a generative aspect of sharing stories of failure, we also recognize that many of our students and colleagues struggle with failure and often try to avoid it at all costs. Fearing or avoiding failure makes sense given how painful (Berns, 2010; von Theinen, Meinel, & Corazza, 2017) and potentially stifling the experiences and emotions associated with failure can be (Beghetto & Dilley, 2016; Tracy & Robins, 2004). This is why simple slogans and platitudes about failure fall short when trying to support a student, colleague, or even ourselves through painful setbacks.

Although it is true that no one really wants to fail or enjoys failure, it is also true that failures can be quite productive and instrumental to learning, creativity, and development (Beghetto, 2022; Kapur, 2016; Manalo & Kapur, 2018). Indeed, there can be unintended consequences (Baert,

1991) that come from our efforts to avoid new actions because we fear a negative outcome. In some cases, it may be more hazardous for learning and development to avoid the risk of failure than to take the risk of trying something new and failing (Beghetto, 2019; Byrnes, 2011).

It has been said that a key to success is knowing when to take a risk (Byrnes, 2011); we would go a step further and suggest that a key to learning and development is also to know how to learn from setbacks and failures. But how might we learn from failures, even painful failures? When young people (or any of us) stumble and fall, we likely will benefit more from a productive way to share and work through those setbacks rather than hearing empty platitudes and pep talks like, "dust yourself off, and try again" or "learn from it and move on."

We recognized that there seems to be a missing moment of reflection, connection, and support that may be helpful in the space between failure and moving forward from that failure. In our work, we realized that sharing stories of failure—particularly if they included details about how it felt and what was learned about the process—could go a long way in establishing a bridge between a setback and learning from that setback. We recognized that specifically highlighting the emotional dimensions of failure in these stories can be an important (and often missing) way of helping young people become aware of and productively work through the wide range of emotions they might experience when they face setbacks in learning and life (Hoffman, Ivcevic, & Maliakkal, 2020).

In this way, stories of failure might serve as both instructive scaffolds (Wood, Bruner, & Ross, 1976) and *emotional scaffolds* (Rosiek & Beghetto, 2009) for young people when encountering their own setbacks. Indeed, students' learning, creativity, and development can be stifled if they do not have the instructive models and supports that can help them productively work through the sometimes profound and negative self-emotions associated with failure (Beghetto & Dilley, 2016; Tracy & Robins, 2004). Such stories, although seemingly helpful, were often shared infrequently.

We then asked, what would happen if we invited people to share stories of failure more systematically (e.g., starting the school year, trying out a new lesson, starting a new collaboration with colleagues, embarking on a new project, or any time people were getting ready to engage in something new, creative, and uncertain)? This book set out to explore this question and took shape in a process where much learning has historically happened—through stories (Bruner, 1991).

We started gathering stories of failures from educators, young people, entrepreneurs, and others about their favorite moment of failure. Through our conversations we uncovered the simple recognition that it is hard to talk about failure. There are few opportunities in our everyday lives to dissect, reflect, and think about how failure can inform and change us. As educators, we believe it is important for young people and everyone else to take creative risks, to try new design ideas.

But how can we support people in taking risks and being creative if we don't front-load honest, vulnerable conversations about our own setbacks? How we might imagine working through those setbacks together and, most importantly, how we intend to bring personal meaning to our taglines about failure?

We invited students, colleagues, and educators to look back on their own failures and think about a favorite failure that they might be willing to share with us. The concept of favorite failure may seem paradoxical at first because failure is never fun. However, we have found that by focusing on favorite failures, it can take some of the edge off of sometimes painful feelings associated with failure and provide a lens for recognizing the learning and the potential gain that can come from experiencing failure. We gathered a wide range of narratives. Although we could not include all of them in this book, we have attempted to showcase stories that highlight key themes, features, and emotions associated with failure. Failures, even painfully embarrassing ones, can lead to new insights about ourselves, situations, and life and even lead to new friendships.

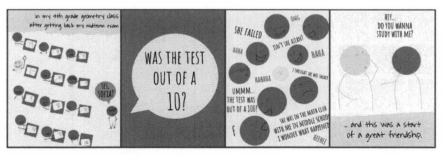

Failure leading to friendship. *Sae Saem Yoon*

Rather than focus on high-level concepts or theories about the features of failure, we collected stories of people's actual experiences with failures. These stories include reflections on how those failures led to shifts—sometimes small and other times large—in how they perceived the world after failure, what they learned, and how we might all learn how to better approach setbacks in our schools, communities, places of work, and everyday lives.

We ultimately wanted to provide educators and young people a range of examples—in an effort to support learning and growth from setbacks. We used the following five-question structure to help provide shape to the stories and support the contributors in taking the beautiful risk of sharing these stories with others (Beghetto, 2019):

1. **Think about a time you tried something new or important and it didn't work out? What happened?** This question helps focus the discussion on specific instances of failure (e.g., failing a math test, trying out for a sports team and not making it, designing your own outfit for a school dance, and so on);

2. **How did it feel when it happened?** This is a critical question as many discussions about failure often avoid discussing the emotional dimensions—particularly negative emotions—that can accompany failure;

3. **What did you learn about that situation?** This question turns the attention to what was learned and gained from the failure. It helps illustrate how even painful setbacks can still be learning opportunities. It also keeps the discussion focused on specific instances of failure (e.g., I learned that I need to spend more time studying and making sure I understand the material; I learned that I should seek assistance and feedback when designing something that will be displayed in public);

4. **What did you learn about yourself?** This question focuses the narrative on the kinds of self-learning and reflection that can result from setbacks. It also highlights how learning and moving forward from failures helps shape our identities as learners and human beings; and

5. **Why is this failure a favorite?** This question helps ensure that the narrative highlights what specifically about this failure resulted in a lasting and positive contribution (e.g., It is my favorite because it has really helped me to be more mindful of the kinds of feedback I provide to students, and so on).

The stories we included in this book help to highlight the nuances, colors, and textures of failure. Like segments of a quilt, these stories are stitched together through the emotions connected to those moments of failure. One story illustrates the intricate nature of perspective. Another demonstrates the vastness and overwhelming power that guilt can play in our pursuit to take bold risks. The others comprise a vibrant fabric of emotions and principles that include: embarrassment, curiosity, honesty, humility, paralysis, expectation, surprise, and disappointment.

Although we highlight a central theme and principle in sharing and discussing each of these stories, we want to underscore that these stories are much richer than any one concept. These are lived stories of setbacks and, taken together, illustrate how difficult setbacks and the full range of emotions and reactions that come from experiencing those setbacks can continually teach us about similar situations, ourselves, and our lives. These stories also offer perspectives and insights on how we can all anticipate, navigate, and incorporate the lessons learned from failure.

WHY READ THIS BOOK?

Why should you, your students, or anyone read this book? One reason is because we don't teach about failure. Educational systems sometimes develop an obsession with success. A successful grade equates to a successful grade point average, which means getting into a successful college with the hope of having a successful and thriving career. We don't teach how to navigate setbacks. We celebrate success and high-achieving students as the beacon of learning, failing repeatedly to examine structures and systems that are failing students and young people today. But what would school, universities, and other places of learning look and feel like if we began each year talking about failure?

We both work at well-established universities where students arrive as having been successful students. They may not have necessarily been satisfied with or even enjoyed their prior learning experiences, but they were successful. They made it through. They succeeded at the game of school (Fried, 2005), but they all experienced setbacks, and the more they take charge of their own learning and lives, they will experience continual rounds of failure, sometimes profound failures. There are also countless students who didn't attain their educational goals, who may feel like they failed or perhaps even view themselves as failures.

We realized if we truly wanted our young people to be more creative, more excited to take risks, iterate, be more emphatic and supportive of other people's setbacks, then it might be helpful to spend time engaging with and sharing their own stories of what it means to have small and sometimes insignificant moments of failure as well as jaw-dropping moments of epic failure. In many K–12 schools and universities, there are moments where students reflect on their learning. These moments take the shape of celebrations of learning, exhibitions, portfolio reviews, and more.

Reflective moments often occur at the end of a project or year. Many of these reflections focus on the stories of their learning, narratives about failure, narratives about the dynamic of teamwork, of failing to meet expectations, narratives that were riddled with the emotions of failure and success. In experiencing these end-of-year reflections, we realized that we just don't need to structure year-end, project-end reflective moments, we need to build the container in all learning environments (formal and informal) where failure is seen as part of the learning process, where real understanding, vulnerability, and willingness to take risks is built from day one.

Inviting and sharing stories of failures from day one requires shifting our commonly held belief that we need to wait to take such risks until we build an environment of trust. We often delay risk-taking until we feel the students are "ready" or can trust us and each other. There is no set date when this can occur. It could be a week, a month, the end of the year. We realized why not just start the year with risk-taking? Doing so can accelerate the development of a trusting environment because it seems that trust comes from taking risks together, rather than the other way around (Grant & Coyle, 2018).

We also realized that when we build trust by taking these kinds of beautiful risks together (Beghetto, 2018, 2019), we can establish the kind of learning environment that provides the emotional and social scaffolding necessary for productively working through and learning from failures (Kapur, 2016). We therefore encourage you to ask, what if you started talking about failure from day one, drawing on stories from this book, bringing in former students to talk about their own failures, and sharing your own stories of failure? Would doing so set the stage for students and educators to build trust and support each other in taking productive risks, working through setbacks, and ultimately learning from the process regardless of the outcome? We hope that by reading this book you will take the next step of sharing and inviting stories of favorite failures with young people.

HOW TO READ AND USE THIS BOOK

You can read this book in whatever way makes sense to you. You can read it cover to cover. Drop in on a chapter. Compare chapters. Use it as a guide to anticipate failure for yourself and others. Revisit the narratives before and after your own and other people's setbacks. Regardless of your approach, we hope you find it as a way of moving beyond superficial platitudes when it comes to the risks involved in learning and life.

Many educators, coaches, and parents often say, "Just try. You'll be okay, you might fail but you'll be okay." As we have mentioned, on the surface and in the moment, such quick pep talks feel right but in reading the stories in this book, we might all come to the realization that such simple encouragements often fall short. One reason they fall short is because they don't address the immediate and long-term impact those moments have on young people—those moments when they actually fail and when they are not okay with the failure.

Failure changes how we see ourselves, how we approach the world, and how we see others. This book is about exploring the fabric of failure, allowing us not only to get more vulnerable about failure ourselves but also to open the conversation about what it feels like to fail and how it changes us. We've tried to encapsulate the fabric of failure, the mosaic of failure not just to understand what failure is but also to shine a light on the nuances around what it means to fail, fail painfully, fail often, and fail toward learning.

The stories in the book are stitched together like a quilt, giving you an overview of the mosaic of failure but also shining a light on the components of failure. The stories provide an insight into how you can create the conditions where you're going to take risks together and then experience failure together. The narratives are from people who examined their favorite failures, pulled the stories apart, and provided us with an opportunity to understand how failure is not just one moment or one set of emotions.

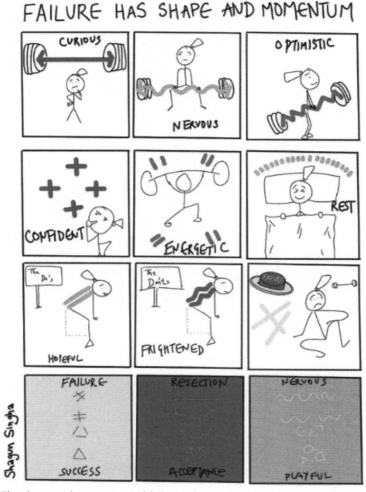

The shape and momentum of failure. *Shagun Singha*

These stories provide us with a glimpse into how we can approach teaching, learning, and setbacks with more humility and more humanity. It's more than just about getting unstuck, because failure has its own shape, its own momentum, and shapes who we are all trying to become.

We have structured each of the 10 chapters in this book as a dialogue between the two of us and the favorite failure narratives. The format is conversational, based on our reactions in dialogue with the narratives and each other. The dialogues in each chapter represent a lightly edited transcript of our recorded conversations about these narratives. Given the conversational nature of the chapter, we make limited use of external sources and references. We include external sources and citations in places where we are drawing on concepts or ideas that have directly influenced our discussion or ideas and concepts that we feel readers may be interested in exploring for further consideration and study. We close with an epilogue, which offers a brief summary of key themes we noticed across the stories and our discussions of those stories.

We invite you to use these narratives and the epilogue as a jumping-off point in your own journey and in support of the learning of others. As you read these narratives, we invite you to choose a chapter that intrigues you, examine the story, and ponder the questions raised by the story in the chapter. We also invite you to consider your own failures in light of the narratives we have curated in this volume as you share your own stories and build your own mosaic around your own and others' favorite failures.

We also invite you to think about how you might collect, share, and curate favorite failures. Digital technologies can be a great way to accomplish this from class to class and year to year (Beghetto, 2021; Lambert & Hessler, 2018). Although there likely will be permissions involved in collecting and sharing such stories, we feel that it is worth the effort involved to establish your own set of stories from your own students and colleagues that you can share from year to year for whatever subject area or projects that you use in your teaching.

We also invite you to adopt, modify, and tailor the five favorite failure questions we introduced above to use for particular subjects (e.g., math class), tasks (e.g., examinations), or life events (learning to drive; applying to art school). How did those failures make you feel and why do you remember them today? Share the stories with your students, discuss them, write them, and use them as a chance to uncover and anticipate the needs of your communities as they take beautiful risks in learning and life. Ultimately, we encourage you to start any new teaching and learning experience with stories of favorite failures. Instead of an icebreaker at the start of a new course or workshop, for instance, what if instead you shared and invited stories of favorite failures?

Chapter One

Expectation

Cynthia Zhou: Original artwork
produced for this book

*It would be much later in life, and at different times in my career, that I
would also come to realize the importance of asking for feedback and/
or understanding expressed and unexpressed expectations in advance
of a performance. Or, one of the greatest lessons I learned, "failure"
creates opportunities for learning and improvement.*

—Charmaine Mercer

Laura: Failure is grounded in the myth of what we expect to achieve from
the failure or what we expect to receive from the success. Both are en-
tangled with expectations, including what other people expect for us and
our own expectations for ourselves. These expectations are a prediction of
how things are going to play out.

Failure is grounded in what we assume will happen. Many of the
challenges we have with failure are due to the expectations we have for
ourselves, the expectations we have for others, and expectations others

have for us. Often, we are unwilling to let go of these expectations. Our expectations become the failure; so, part of learning from the failure is unraveling and disconnecting the experience from the expectation.

Our moments of success are also grounded in expectations. Part of the reason why our moments of success feel so successful is because they meet our expectations. They may surprise us, but at minimum they meet our expectations. They don't fall short of them.

How can we create moments in classrooms where we let go of expectations and think about what we are learning without connecting the experience to our hard and concrete expectations about how a learning experience might go?

Ron: Yes, I think there's something powerful here about expectations. I love how you're describing how failure is like an expectation gap.

Viewed in this way, failure really is not necessarily about a person, but it's about not being able to accurately predict what's going to happen, so there's like this expectation gap. That's what failure is. It really has nothing to do with your merit as a person, but really, it's just a sign that we, as humans, aren't very good at predicting our own or others' behavior in the future.

I think this is the same as planning a lesson or anything in life. As educators, we design and plan lessons and we have an expectation for how they will go. And if we go off the lesson plan, go "off track," then all of a sudden, we feel like the lesson was a failure, when, in reality, it might be a really powerful learning moment or opportunity.

Going off script can be some of the most powerful learning and teaching moments, but I think we're afraid to do that because we believe that success is about aligning what we anticipated or expected with what happens. There's something very problematic about that because it makes us turn inward and feel bad about ourselves or our capabilities. Or maybe the moment disappoints us, or we disappoint ourselves.

So, this whole idea that expectations are these fixed things is an idea that the stories in this book challenge because if expectations and outcomes don't align (and they often don't), we can learn from those moments. But if we hold on to these expectations, then we get stuck in failure.

What I really like about this story that's coming up is it highlights the role of individual and team expectations in failure and what can be learned from it.

Even though we can learn from failure, there can still be a lot of pain, regret, frustration, and resentment; but, sometimes, we can realize "Oh, okay, there's something else here. Maybe it was just that my expectations weren't aligned."

So, if we can let go of or loosen up those expectations, or at least allow ourselves to realize that our expectations aren't always going to match the experience, then maybe we can see these misalignments not necessarily as fixed failures but as learning opportunities.

Laura: How can we let go of expectations, so that we are able to decouple failure with the outcomes?

Much of schooling defines success as a good grade or making the team. Failure looks like not getting a good grade, not making the team because we see the outcome of an experience as fixed judgment. We view success and failure as binary outcomes, not a spectrum of learning.

I see it across the board—we focus on what is going to be the outcome, then we put a label on it: this was successful, that was a failure. But we spend very little time asking what we learned from the experience.

It's really interesting to me that when I think about expectations in schools, or an organization, so much is focused on the question: Is this going to work? We're going to do this initiative because it will be successful with our young people. While those are laudable aspirations, how can we shift our thinking to focus on what we are learning from these moments?

Can we actually be brave enough to let go of success and failure and release ourselves from the expectation and ask the question, what are we really learning about these experiences? I think we jump so quickly to the dichotomy of: *Was this a success? Was it a failure?* What if instead we remind ourselves to focus on understanding the learning behind what we are doing (whether it is a success or a failure)? The following favorite failure story illustrates some of these ideas about expectations and can help remind us that the focus should be on the learning.

EXPECTATION: MY FAVORITE FAILURE

By Charmaine Mercer

My freshman year in high school I tried out for the junior varsity cheer-leading team. My best friend and I were thrilled to audition together. For weeks, we practiced our choreographed routine at each other's houses after school and during lunch with the other girls who were trying out. Straight backs, hands cupped, from the pelvis, we chanted "JOHN MUIR. IS HERE TO CHEER!" Our rhythm and precision were excellent, accord-ing to the girls who we were trying out with and almost everyone who saw us practice. My best friend and I felt confident we would be chosen for the only two spots available on the JV team that year.

The tryouts were on a Friday, after school, in the boys' basketball gym. We were required to perform a routine we had been taught as a full squad. The team performance was followed by choreographed routines created by groups of two. We stood next to each other during the bigger performance and secretly encouraged each other to do our best using our peripheral vision. We were the last duo to go, and we executed beautifully in our clapping, chanting, and stomping. Once we completed our routine and waited in the hall for the names of the chosen, I recall the butterflies swarming but I was excited.

The next thing I remember were the salty tears and shaking shoulders that resulted from my uncontrollable sobbing, as the captain of the team called names other than ours. We were devastated! I was a complete wreck! I couldn't imagine why we hadn't been chosen! We practiced so hard and did a really great job! I was even more confused when class-mates and teachers shared shock and surprise that we were not chosen. For weeks, I resented the two girls who were chosen, especially because their routine lacked the "rhythm and soul" that ours did. I thought the purpose of cheerleading was to display rhythm and for everyone to like your performance; what did we miss?

It would take me until the second semester of my junior year before I received the answer. It would take me two years before I would try out again. During tryout practice for the varsity cheerleading squad, one day the captain shared how she had been observing how well I performed and that she thought I would be a great cheerleader. A few days later she would make a similar statement, so I finally asked why I had not been chosen two years earlier. She shared that although my friend and I were great performers, we did not lend our talents to the betterment of the team. She went on to share that during the group performance at tryouts, the judges felt the two of us stood out as individuals, which hurt the team's overall performance.

That was when it hit me. I realized that cheerleading was a team sport, and my best friend and I were not viewed as girls who wanted to be a part of a team. We were perceived as people who wanted to be individual stars, not people who wanted to join a team to learn from and to contribute to. As she walked away, she mumbled, "There is no 'I' in team."

I took from this experience that the whole is always greater than its individual parts. I discovered that having an outstanding individual performance that eclipses the shine of the team makes me and the team less effective. It would be much later in life, and at different times in my career, that I would also come to realize the importance of asking for feedback and/or understanding expressed and unexpressed expectations in advance of a performance. Or, one of the greatest lessons I learned—"failure" creates opportunities for learning and improvement. It's crazy when I think about it. An experience I had at 15 years old is the gift that keeps giving in terms of life lessons!

—Charmaine Mercer is a program officer in Education at the William and Flora Hewlett Foundation. Her portfolio focuses on school district transformation and leadership development. Charmaine previously worked as an education director, researcher, and policy specialist for various DC-based nonprofits, and she has held various positions on Capitol Hill, including senior staffer for the House Committees on Appropriations and Education and Labor, and the Congressional Research Service. She is a native Californian and the shamelessly proud mom of adorable twin boys.

Ron: Having read this story, let's go back to your point, Laura, about if it's about learning then there's always an unexpected element, otherwise there's no learning.

If you already know what's going to happen or know something, then how can you possibly learn? So, in a very real way, learning is all about moving from the expected to the unexpected and being able and willing to step into the unexpected.

And, like you mentioned, what often holds us back from even trying sometimes is we don't let go of our expectations. So, expectations can be really paralyzing, both before taking action and after taking action.

Sometimes, before we act, expectations can freeze us into inaction because we might imagine all these terrible outcomes and we're afraid to even try.

Or when we do act, but it doesn't meet our or others' expectations, we feel the pain of that gap. But what if we shifted away from that and moved towards learning? Doing so requires us to kind of engage with the unexpected.

This kind of goes against a lot of the received wisdom of education, which stresses the importance of having and clarifying expectations so that we can ensure that we and our students meet those expectations.

But, based on what we've been exploring in our conversation about expectations, that would mean that there's really no learning happening because if everyone knows clearly what's expected and knows exactly how to do that, then what learning really has happened? It just becomes a demonstration of what you already know.

So, I think there's some interesting ideas here to wrestle with about how we can allow more space for the unexpected and give less power and energy to the expected.

I think that's where the real challenging reflection question is that comes out of this story, and all these stories in this book, and that question is: What if we only learn, deeply learn, when we engage with the unexpected part of an experience, even if it is a painful experience?

Laura: I love that the story comes from a powerful individual, but the story also helps question the difference between individual and group expectations.

This story is about learning and growth. As educators, how do we dance between high expectations and a culture of inquiry and curiosity?

It is very common to say that we must have high expectations of students in our classrooms. We create rubrics that articulate very clearly what those expectations might be. In the best-case scenarios, those expectations are cocreated by students and teachers. Even in the best of cases when expectations are cocreated, we create expectations around failure and success and pay little attention to what we learn from those experiences.

As the cofounder of High Tech High, Rob Riordon was always very cautious about using rubrics because they set up this false binary around learning that suggested students either met or did not meet expectations. These strict rubric levels of performance did not leave a lot of opportunity for conversation.

As educators, when we design a new unit or project, we have expectations about learning outcomes we think we are covering; but in reality, we can never really know what else students might learn from the projects. Yes, there might be a met expectation around learning a new content standard, but the deeper skills around collaboration, passion, or communication often come out in unexpected ways that the rubric could not predict. How do we make space for the unexpected outcomes in learning?

Ron: Even if we must use a certain set of rubrics or there are certain sets of predetermined expectations, can we also design a space in those rubrics for the unexpected? This way we're not limited by expectations. If all we do is try to meet expectations, we're going to miss out on so many learning opportunities.

In the story there's this idea of the expressed and unexpressed expectations. I think that's a good place to start for educators: What are the expressed and unexpressed expectations in our classrooms?

When unexpected things happen, how can we talk through them and learn from them, because it seems like where much of the interesting learning is happening is in the unexpected.

Unexpressed expectations are crucial to uncover. As this story shows, unexpressed expectations can be painful, particularly when you're a young person and you're trying out for something.

Your identity may be wrapped up in what you're trying to do or become whether it is a cheerleader, a member of a team or academic club, or whatever. When we don't meet those expectations, we have this opportunity to work through the expectation gap and learn from that process.

Laura: It is also important for us to think about the invisible or the visible expectations we set in our classrooms and how they are inherently connected to race and identity. What's expected behavior and what's not expected? How does race and identity influence what is deemed expected behavior?

How do we open our classroom and ourselves up to multiple ways of being and knowing and start removing the simple dichotomy of success or failure that's wrapped up in our very outdated network of school systems?

How can we start to see how this outdated model of success versus failure is *actually* failing our young people—particularly students who have been historically marginalized?

How can we unstack the deck and discover multiple ways of reflecting on our learning that moves from the binary idea of success and failure toward a spectrum of possibilities to uncover learning?

Ron: Absolutely—forced conformity and sameness privileges sameness and so, if you do have the same or shared social, cultural, and historical background as your teacher, that's kind of already an unexpressed expectation that privileges certain identities and races.

How can we embrace the unexpected, which allows us to be open to difference and to recognize that there are different ways of meeting criteria, *and* still do quality work? We must let go of these fixed expectations that really are just markers of sameness, rather than opportunities for creativity and different ways of knowing and expressing.

The most beautiful teaching moments are when teachers get surprised and peers get surprised at what everyone can do together, do differently, and still do high-quality work. Expectations are such a huge buzzword in education: high expectations and meet expectations and clear expectations.

This story reveals, however, that there is a different way of viewing expectations. How might we let go of those expectations so we can prioritize learning?

What expectations are we holding on to that are impeding our opportunities to learn from and with each other?

Chapter Two

Frozen

Cynthia Zhou: Original artwork
produced for this book

*The first 30 seconds went well, but . . . suddenly, I forgot my speech. I
wanted to cry with embarrassment.*

—Mihyun Han, PhD

Ron: Okay, we're not talking about the Disney movie in this chapter, but
the feeling of being frozen in a moment of failure. There may be some
parallels with the movie. But, the favorite failure story in this section really
invites us to revisit what happens and what can be learned from freezing
up either right before an event or in the midst of an event or experience.

It's the idea of how we can find ourselves immobilized because we're
spending so much energy processing what's going on that we are not able
to think or act in the way we want, imagined, or prepared ourselves to act.

We see a lot of these moments in schools when students are being
asked to present something, particularly during "cold calls" from teachers asking them to read a new passage aloud, respond to a question, or
solve a problem on the board. Even if we have prepared for the speech

or practiced the math problem, everything starts to disappear and we're frozen in the moment.

These moments have this intense social component to them. Where everything's frozen, the audience is frozen as well. This raises questions about the moment itself but also how we can use reflection and anticipation to help young people, our colleagues, and ourselves get unfrozen in those moments. How can we unfreeze ourselves and others in such moments? What can we learn from freezing?

These are intense and often surprising moments because they seem so different from learning, which often feels very cognitive. It is more than an embarrassment. Freezing is a whole-body experience, where everything stops, except for the expectation that something is supposed to be moving forward.

Laura: There's something palpable about being in the middle of a failure moment and feeling frozen about what to do or where to go next. The next story reminds us that these frozen moments happen in front of others.

We easily notice when these frozen moments happen to someone else. We can understand them. We can connect with them because we've all seen and probably have been frozen before.

The young woman in the story is an English Language Learner. As a former English as Second Language teacher, there were lots of moments where I saw young people become frozen icicles in the classroom because they were unsure of what to say next. They are thinking about what to say, translating, all the while filled with the potential dread of simply not knowing the answer.

How do we get better at noticing the icicles as they're forming through the emotions and faces of the young people that we are working with? What's our individual and collective responsibility to others and our students when they are becoming frozen? How can we get better at anticipating and showing up for our students during these riskful moments? My hunch is that if we get better at anticipating and reflecting on these beautiful, risky moments, we will accumulate a better way to get unstuck.

Ron: This next story really raises so many questions about what's going on when we or others freeze in big and small ways. It gets me thinking about how that freezing moment can make us feel completely alone. And how, in those moments, we feel the gaze of the audience, but interestingly the audience also is feeling frozen.

Maybe we need to anticipate the possibility of these moments both for ourselves and, even more importantly, as an audience member. How can we create multiple ways to exit out of those moments? How can we notice them early, see those micro-icicles forming?

Perhaps it is giving people an option to demonstrate their learning differently. Instead of a whole group presentation, maybe it is a small group first. Or perhaps a student brings up a peer who is willing to simply stand by them. There is a collective responsibility, an emerging ethos: We can unfreeze those moments together if we simply get better at noticing and anticipating moments of failure.

How can we help ourselves and others disrupt those moments—establishing learning environments where this commitment becomes a shared responsibility?

FROZEN: MY FAVORITE FAILURE

By Mihyun Han, PhD

Here is one unforgettable failure of mine that I experienced in the language research conference held a couple of years ago. At the time, I was working on a research study that explored English Learners' language learning emotions. I was interpreting the data collected, which seemed interesting enough to share with others. I was deeply motivated to share the initial research findings with the language research community.

When reading the call-for-proposals announcement, I found out that the conference had a new research-sharing event that they just launched, called "Data Blitz." Data Blitz was a two-minute presentation opportunity where selected presenters could quickly share their research project's gist with other conference attendees.

Considering the limitations that poster presentations had—you can share your research with a limited number of random people who are passing by your poster–the Data Blitz event looked very appealing to me. So, without hesitation, I applied to present my research study in the poster session and the Data Blitz session.

Early morning on the conference day, I hung my poster on the wall and spent the two-hour poster session actively sharing my research project with the conference attendees. It was before noon when the Data Blitz event was about to begin. While sitting in the first row of the large conference hall waiting for the event to start, I felt good.

More accurately speaking, I felt confident and prepared since I had spent quite many hours writing a perfect presentation script and rehearsing the two-minute presentation with a stopwatch timing it. But before long, my confidence began to crack. I found out that all other Data Blitz presenters except me were carrying either a script paper or a set of small index cards in their hands. My heart started pounding. I realized that I was the only empty-handed presenter. And this bad feeling was never wrong. My 2-minute Data Blitz presentation began in about 10 minutes, and I ended up spending 15 seconds of it, a relatively significant portion of the time, staring blankly into the air.

The first 30 seconds went well, but after then, suddenly, I forgot my speech. I wanted to cry with embarrassment in front of the hundreds of the audience.

Then something unexpected happened. The audience, who were being quiet with a look of faint surprise on their faces, all at once began to applaud. The audience's cheers and applause echoed gently but warmly in the conference hall, and they helped me calm down and catch my breath. I let go of the planned script lines tangled in my head. I presented the main points of my research as I recall, and the remaining one minute went by really fast. Anyway, I was able to finish my Data Blitz presentation.

Yet, as soon as I got off the lectern, the overwhelming feelings of disappointment and embarrassment raced through me. Why did I ruin the presentation that everyone else completed successfully without any problems? A sense of remorse for not being more fully prepared rushed in as well.

While I was mentally processing those complicated feelings as I reviewed the situation one by one, I recognized two things that I overlooked in the preparation process. First, as a participant who was going to present in a newly launched research-sharing event, I should have been equipped with more information about the opportunity, such as where the new event would be held and how many people I would be facing in the presentation.

Second, I should have been aware of my bilingual self in the preparation process: the negative emotions that I could have possibly experienced by participating in the risky event where I was supposed to share my ideas and thoughts in my second language, English. During the presentation, the hundreds of the audience's eyes were on me, which indeed overwhelmed my feelings.

Research has shown that language learners can experience various negative emotions in the situation where their second language use can be judged and evaluated. Unexpectedly presenting in front of a large number of people in my second language, I experienced negative emotions such as embarrassment, anxiety, and fear, which directly caused me to lose speech in the middle of the presentation.

Ironically, this experience of mine in the new presentation event reassured my research findings, the key content that my Data Blitz presentation was supposed to deliver: The English Language students in the college classroom experienced various negative emotions to express their creative ideas in their second language. Many of the students shared their expectations of teacher emotional support, which they viewed as enabling them to take a risk and share more creative ideas.

I call this unsuccessful presentation of mine in the new two-minute Data Blitz event my favorite failure. I would not have experienced this failure if I had presented only in the safe poster presentation session and avoided participating in the new presentation activity. The presentation did not go as I had expected, yet I somehow earned a valuable opportunity to share the results of my research study with more people.

This experience provided me with some valuable new insights on how to emotionally support students who are learning in new situations and experiencing failures, as demonstrated in the audience's cheering applause and the positive effect on me. These insights that I gained by participating in the new expressive opportunity led me to reflect on how learning happens regarding how failures can make a lasting contribution to expanding individuals' knowledge and experiences. As a teacher educator, I am pleased to have a practical experience that I can share with my students to discuss how to view failures from the educator's perspective.

—Mihyun Han is an assistant professor at Hope College in Michigan. Mihyun teaches literacy education and ESL/bilingual education, and creativity development for all students is her favorite topic to discuss. Recently Mihyun's research has revolved around bilingual/ ELL student creativity development and their emotional well-being in education settings.

Laura: Being frozen seems to be the body's visceral reaction to sensing embarrassment and shame.

After reading this story, I'm struck by a couple things. First, the audience noticed she was frozen and, in that moment, chose to warmly applaud her.

The audience reaction was beautiful. It reinforced my belief in our collective humanity. This story raises questions about what happens before and during a moment of failure, but one of the simplest things this story teaches us is the provocation to ask: How did that feel?

When we're reflecting on learning, it's important to ask how that experience felt. Instead of engaging first in conversations about the content, the assessment or group project, start with the question of: How did that feel?

By asking that question two things happen. First, we can begin to see how people are reacting to the learning. We hear the emotions that this experience evoked. Second, it can reveal cultural biases we hold. Getting on stage for some people might feel less scary, but as an emerging bilingual person this moment was doubly scary.

How can we use that question of how did it feel to really uncover not just the content that young people are exploring but the cultural ramifications of the work that we're doing? How can it help us better understand how to create culturally responsive classrooms?

Ron: Such an important set of questions, Laura. I love your question of "how did that feel?" I love this question because, by inviting emotions into the classroom, even negative emotions (like that felt terrible, that was horrible), we are providing a deeper level of support for students. We are recognizing that learning is sometimes painful, frustrating, and, most importantly, human.

It's strange that usually the only emotions welcome in the classroom are positive emotions. How can students who are feeling the painful emotions of setbacks that come from learning feel supported if they are allowed only to show and experience positive emotions?

By inviting different perspectives and experiences as part of an assigned reflection, we can help demonstrate that learning and creative insights can benefit from engaging with difference. It suggests that it is okay to have an experience different from what others experienced, even if it includes freezing up in a moment. Maybe being open to differences can help the unfreezing process? Perhaps this can also be part of the way we help ourselves and others anticipate and prepare for different experiences and emotional reactions with learning events we plan and participate in?

I also love the applause in this story. One takeaway or metaphor for ourselves and our students is: Will you be the first person to clap when you see somebody freezing? It's easy to be the second person to clap, but somebody had to have the awareness and willingness to start clapping and to shatter the frozen moment.

That's a beautiful risk because the presentation wasn't done, but it was able to continue after that applause. These are the moments we hope to see in classrooms. Whether it is starting to applaud or standing up to a bully who is picking on another child, it asks the question: Who is going to take the brave risk of disrupting that moment? Who has the courage to clap first to shatter the frozen state?

Laura: Yes. Who is the person that's going to turn the heater on in freezing moments and make it warmer again—literally and figuratively for the person who is stuck?

One of the insights we're learning from this story, and others, is that failure is often viewed as an individual act but that failure is a communal experience. Most stories of failure are often told in isolation. Failure feels isolating. We say "I failed," but in actuality it is a community experience.

We think failure is something that one person does, but this story reminds us that failure and success are not solo acts. We can turn a moment of failure into a successful experience when we anticipate it and rely on a community of learners to stand by us when we get stuck.

If failure is communal, then it reminds us that we have opportunity and responsibility to step in and care for each other when failure is occurring.

Ron: This shared responsibility may be one of if not *the* most important and powerful messages of this entire book. It's such a powerful message to realize that although individuals often get blamed in these moments or labeled as being the failure or they put the blame on themselves, maybe it's really a failure of the entire social environment.

And in the case of this story, the social environment didn't fail! The audience did not fail the author of this story, but easily could have. Someone in that audience realized that what they were experiencing was a shared failure and a shared responsibility to move forward from it.

Instead of putting the failure spotlight on one person, the spotlight needs to expand to shed light on the collective responsibility during moments of failure. This, of course, doesn't mean that there are no individual responsibilities, but from the vantage point of an educator, maybe we can cultivate shared responsibility in the learning environment so that when people are taking beautiful risks in front of us, and stumbling, we can all support them and not fail them?

Chapter Three

Curiosity

Cynthia Zhou: Original artwork
produced for this book

I took the risk of being myself.

—Mariia Vitrukh

Ron: Curiosity is a word I don't usually associate with failure. I have typically viewed curiosity as what might lead us to some action or experience that can result in a failure, like exploring a new topic.

When exploring a new interest, for example, we try it out and maybe have a setback. But what's interesting about this upcoming story is how curiosity serves as the driver for working through failures.

Curiosity, in this way, is a persistent driver of trying to understand, learn from, and work through failures. In this way it fuels the willingness to sit with and work through failure, even if you feel like your confidence has been shattered.

This is a fresh way of thinking about curiosity and its relationship to failure.

There's a lot of slogans about failure like "have grit" and persist through your failures, but such slogans fall short because they don't give us the reason why or how we should or could persist through the pain of failure.

These slogans also do not recognize that sometimes the healthiest or successful thing to do might be to step away from something and modify it or do something else. And, of course, there are times when persisting is so important, but doing so doesn't necessarily get at the basis of why we would want to persist.

Persistence in some cases can seem like dwelling in endless pain and hopelessness. If you are facing a seemingly insurmountable obstacle to where you want to go and you believe you will never get there, then why would you persist? So, the idea is that curiosity might be one reason why you would want to persist—curiosity about exploring and learning from the situation.

Simply being curious about what we have just experienced, sitting with what we are currently experiencing, and exploring movement in different and new directions may open a new horizon of possibilities for our learning lives.

In the case of the story we will be exploring, it is about a person whose curiosity fueled persistence through so many setbacks and toward realization of a goal.

Laura: This got me thinking, what is persistence? Is it curiosity? And I think you just touched on it. We hear a lot about a growth mindset versus fixed mindset (Dweck, 2000), but we actually never think about the role curiosity plays in working through failure.

A growth mindset is important, but curiosity might be what helps students persist through failure. I think much of our educational system views persistence as an equivalent for hard work. Failing while doing boring, hard work is somehow a prerequisite to success. If a student is working hard and not curious about what they are learning, then it might actually feel like torture.

As an educational designer I think a lot about what we are asking students to get curious about so that the curiosity can sustain them through the setbacks. Sadly, though, I am sure I have given my students assignments that weren't focused on sparking students' curiosity. I wanted them to learn the content standards; not spark their curiosity.

I recall having said things such as "You should learn this standard because one day it will help you in real life." And while that may or may not have been true, the premise of the project was not grounded in what students were interested in.

If we are going to help all young people and ourselves become lifelong learners, we need to be curious about our failures.

This next story helps us think about how we can use curiosity as the fuel to discover moments of failure. When our failures are devoid of curiosity or ambiguity, then it is no wonder that our young people don't want to fail because it's not interesting to fail. There's nothing to learn.

If we want our students to develop a growth mindset, then we need to provide opportunities for them to reflect on what they are learning, what they are getting better at, and what questions emerge for them.

As educators, we often decide even before we meet our students what they need to be interested in. Then we expect them to persevere through those learning moments. How can we become more curious about what we are teaching and why? How can we understand what makes our students curious and help them see their failures through their own curiosity? Perhaps by grounding our assignments in what makes our students curious will sustain them through setbacks.

Curiosity about learning and curiosity about what's on the other side of that failure provide us with the urge to know more. Curiosity helps us push through because possibility sits on the other side.

In this next story, the author is curious about if it is possible to have the kind of experience that she was hoping for, if she could just push through this failure then she can see what is on the other side of it: a new experience for me, a new life for me, a new identity . . . who knows, right? Maybe curiosity is what's really driving that urge to keep going despite the failure and to discover something about ourselves, about the content, what we're capable of doing.

CURIOSITY: MY FAVORITE FAILURE

By Mariia Vitrukh

Most of the time you are alone in your risks and rewards of failing. Although there are supportive friends, family, or colleagues, you live through those creative probes, sleepless nights, and sour pains by yourself.

It was my fifth year applying for a master's program abroad and 26 failed applications: rejected, partially funded, or not funded. Bitter taste of "We regret to inform you . . .": I swallowed my pride and shattered self-confidence again and approached the blank drawing board.

Now or never, I thought to myself. Working on average three jobs as an English teacher and translator in Ukraine, I knew that another round of applications would cost me a fortune.

What was intrinsically driving me? Curiosity! Creative search and a wish to transform learning experiences I had as a student. An urge to know if it was possible to have an inspiring and collaborative learning environment in an inherited post-Soviet teacher-centered context.

I sketched my passions: my mental drawing board was swirling with uncertainty and risks in writing, in ideas, in lines of thought, and in experiences. Études of bits and pieces, creative encounters and procrastinations, experiments, perspectives, theories, and visions.

Art school application. *Mariia Vitrukh*

I took the risk of being myself on the application pages.

"I would like to congratulate you on your selection for a scholarship at the University of Cambridge," I read eight months later. "Your study is supported by the Open Society Foundations and the University of Cambridge." I was the only one selected in social sciences. One out of six selected from the whole country.

It was my 27th application. I had never received a better award for failing. Never before had I felt so much myself either.

—Mariia is a doctoral student at Arizona State University.

Laura: At the end of the story the author mentions that she never received a better award for failing—which was to succeed on the 27th application. So what kind of questions does this story raise for us as educators?

There's something about the 27th time. Not 5 applications, or 10 or 20. But 27 applications!

There was risk of not only financial loss, but also personal risk. The relentless curiosity drove this persistence.

Curiosity is a natural trait. Humans by nature are curious people (Glăveanu, 2020). A few questions to consider might be:

- What are you curious about?
- What are you looking to discover?
- What do you need to understand more when you think about the needs of young people?
- How can you empathize more?
- How can you bring your own curiosities into the design of learning experiences?

These questions help us discover what we are curious about. It's not about predicting what our young people need, but really getting curious about what is possible.

Ron: Yes, I really like this, Laura. How can we find ways to not only be curious about the design process but also stay curious enough to take risks to design curricula that do not have fixed ends? It seems to me that purposefully maintaining some unknown elements in the design can be generative.

What if we allowed ourselves to not know how this activity, this project, the assignment will turn out because the students are driving it?

If we really turn over or open aspects of the design to allow students to drive it then we can't know every aspect in advance. Maybe then we will have a real opportunity to be curious about how it will turn out? And, perhaps, this curiosity will enable us to persist through the setbacks.

This story also invites us to think about parallels to our own work as educators. For example, what if you teach a lesson 26 times, but every time it's a terrible experience for you and your students? Maybe we can still be curious about how we can find a way to make the lesson work. This may be particularly important if it's a topic that you're required to teach. Rather than just give into the idea that this is a "boring" or unfulfilling lesson, you can keep working on it, keep redesigning it.

I think we have to be curious about the possibilities of how things can turn out. Otherwise, it may be easy to just approach it as something to get through on the path to something more interesting.

There's another statement in the story that I found very compelling. It was when the author explained, "I took the risk of being myself." This seemed like a breakthrough. I think educators eventually realize that we need to bring our uniqueness to the teaching, we can't simply try to mimic all our past teachers. This kind of risk-taking, coupled with curiosity about our own and students' failures, seems so important for success and can maybe help us learn through and from the failures and setbacks along the way.

The insights from this story raise such interesting questions, such as:

- How can we help support young people in being curious about and taking the risk of being themselves?
- How can we as educators take the risk of being curious about who we are and can be as educators?
- What if when we're thinking about designing learning experiences, we not only design with curiosity, but also try to design with the curiosity about ourselves and our students to allow young people and ourselves to learn about who we really are and can be as part of the process?

Laura: I love the idea of getting curious about ourselves. And I really applaud the author's willingness to go through the process 27 times. I'm wondering now about what resulted from that experience. Is this about an achievement? Or was this about getting curious about herself and her own ability as an artist?

I think the piece that's important for us as educators to hold on to as we entertain this concept of failure is being curious about the needs of our young people, the needs of our community, and the needs of our society and being willing to sometimes let go of a particular outcome.

In design, we often talk about parallel prototyping (Dow, 2010)—lots of possible solutions—designing multiple pathways to success that leverage divergent thinking. For me, that is an important part of curiosity—it's about getting curious about the different pathways.

Parallel possibilities that invite multiple ways of knowing may also better serve students who have been historically underserved and underinvested in our education system. If we are to better serve our Black, Indigenous, and other young people of color, we need to acknowledge what we do not know and be curious about their social, emotional, cultural, and contextual needs.

If a teacher has lost the curiosity to learn about and understand their students and the topics they are teaching, I am not sure we can create quality learning experiences.

How do we cultivate more curiosity? How do we transition the power in a classroom where everyone is curious about an area of exploration? How can we design experiences where curiosity can live and breathe in its most authentic form, without being confined by the predetermined learning outcomes?

It takes a bold educator to release themselves from these confines. But when educators do this, it seems like it can lead to boundless curiosity and the opportunity to learn alongside young people.

Ron: You raise such important questions and considerations for us, Laura! I also want to briefly highlight this idea of being curious enough to shift our attention away from a solitary focus on attaining predetermined learning outcomes and toward being more curious about to-be-determined possibilities of working with and learning from the young people who are gathered in the classroom.

What are the possibilities that can be realized from encouraging and taking the risk of being yourself as a student, an educator, a human being in schools, classrooms, and beyond?

What if we designed openings in the learning experience that allowed us all to be curious about differences and what can be learned together from not only pursuing student interests, but learning from the setbacks and failures along the way?

Chapter Four

Disappointment

Cynthia Zhou: Original artwork
produced for this book

*Truth be told, "favorite" is an adjective I can use only in hindsight.
Failing was not fun or ever a favorite thing, at the time.*

—Punya Mishra

Laura: This next story is about disappointment. We haven't talked a lot about how disappointing failure can be personally or publicly, but some failures can really rip at your soul and identity.

When we think about disappointment as it relates to failure, there is the moment itself that can feel disappointing because of the expectation around what was supposed to happen. Then, there is a deeper disappointment that goes beyond the moment. The deeper disappointment is in the idea that you are not capable, that you are not cut out for this, and you start thinking you are not the person who you thought you were supposed to be.

This deeper disappointment around failure is revealing. It shines a light on our talents, our gifts. And that can be disappointing because we have an idea of who we're supposed to be based on stories, our identities, and the expectations of the context we were raised in, the race and gender we hold, and the communities we live in. These stories set up a narrative in our mind about who we're supposed to be.

Then we have a moment of failure that unravels us, and we are disappointed because we don't meet the expectations of our own stories. This is an utter disappointment. It is not just the failure of not succeeding or making the grade or meeting the moment, but a deep disappointment in ourselves.

The disappointment is twofold. First is the disappointment in ourselves. Then there are disappointing realizations about the system(s) we grew up with that made us believe in these now untrue stories.

It is the disappointment that systems or structures we grew up with were never designed with us in mind at all. The system never saw you to begin with. So you feel disappointed in yourself and you feel disappointed in the system. You might even feel disappointed in the people who contributed to creating the now untrue, unraveled beliefs about yourself; so the disappointment cuts across yourself, others, and the context.

This can lead to anger, sadness, isolation, and, rightfully so, rebellion.

When we think about disappointment, it raises an important and difficult question: What are we really disappointed about when we think about failure? Are we disappointed in ourselves, disappointed that the moment did not meet our expectations, or is it disappointment in the system and the structures that made us think we could succeed?

Ron: The ideas that you're discussing bring out this multifaceted experience of disappointment. As I was listening to you talk about this and thinking about the story in this section, I realized there is part of disappointment that is about not meeting expectations . . . failing to arrive at what you hoped for in yourself, or what you hoped for in the experience, or even what other people hoped for you to be or do in a situation. This all ties back to the first chapter and story in the book on expectation, but it adds additional texture and variations around the experience of disappointment in relation to failure.

All of these disappointments are illustrated in the story featured in this chapter. It's about having a profoundly unsatisfying experience— specifically a gap between who we think we are and who we want *to be* at that moment.

It is about losing hope in what was expected and the profound sadness that can come with it. And, yes, there's kind of a deep sadness, particularly if it's a prolonged disappointment . . . a sadness that can be really brutal: self-disappointment, disappointment in other people, disappointment with the entire situation and the narrowing sensation of losing hope.

But there's also this important relationship between disappointment and hope that we often don't think, hear, or talk much about. It's about how hope is something that can be lost, but also something that can be found and bring us out of failure into learning. And how, when failure is a prolonged experience, it can really be difficult to recover from.

Laura: As we think about disappointment in our personal experiences, be they as a student or as an educator, there's this connection between disappointment and hope. Part of the challenge we're facing in education is the often disappointing hope for something better.

Our young people show up to a classroom where they might have spent 10 hours over the weekend working on a project they're really excited about to show. They hope the teacher will like what they have done. They are eager to show us and others what they have done. They hope that their presentation will go well. And then there's a deep disappointment when it doesn't meet the expectations, when it does not go well, or when it doesn't work and whatever hope the work carried is lost.

Prolonged disappointment can result in disengagement, particularly in high schools.

By the time some students get to high school, many of their hopes about school have been slashed many times over. They may have hoped to fit it, to feel a sense of belonging, to find a new friend, or to discover a teacher that likes them.

At the start of each year, there is always a small glimmer of hope that this year is going to be better; "this teacher is going to believe in me"; "I'm going to do better" . . . but if we are continuing to create experiences in our classroom that don't allow our young people to feel like their full selves are being valued, then that glimmer of hope can be lost.

When we implement oppressive structures that marginalize our most underserved students or when we utilize outdated, biased, or racist discipline practices, we squash the hope that this year was going to be different. Not only do we harm curiosity and devalue students' identities, we crush their hopes that learning could be better. If we do not provide opportunities for all young people to express their unique talents and gifts in different ways, we create a system that protects and values prolonged disappointment.

So, this next story is about the relationship between disappointment and hope, and it raises some really profound questions for us all, including: What are the expectations and potential disappointments we're creating in our classrooms? Are the learning opportunities we design crushing the hope of our young people?

DISAPPOINTMENT: MY FAVORITE FAILURE

By Punya Mishra

The "favorite" failure that I always keep going back to is an extended one—stretching across the four years I spent in the undergraduate program in engineering, back in India. Truth be told, "favorite" is an adjective I can use only in hindsight. Failing was not fun or ever a favorite thing, at the time.

Just to give some context, in high school I was a highly enthusiastic, motivated kid. I read a lot, across the board— science, technology, mathematics, literature, film, you name it. I simply wanted to learn. Though I was partial towards science, and physics in particular, at some level it did not matter what the topic was. I had a vision of becoming a physicist when I grew up, studying the very small (e.g., quarks) or the very large (e.g., galaxies).

The challenge was that in India, if you were good at (or vaguely amenable to) science and math, you become either an engineer or a doctor. These were the choices offered, so I ended up in an engineering college, and that was that.

Sadly, however, I did not enjoy my four years in engineering at all. It was all about exams and quizzes, nonstop, with an all-encompassing focus on rote learning. There was no space or time for understanding or playing with ideas. I remember, in my first semester, in a class on quantum physics, I was writing limericks and poems about the ideas I was learning in the class. Imagine poems (bad ones) about wave particle duality, quantum states, and the periodic table of elements. These poems were just my way of playing with ideas—similar to how a cat will play with a ball of yarn. These forays were purposeless in some way, yet meaningful in others. But sadly, that impulse to play was squelched quite quickly, partly because it was not valued and partly because there was not any time for it, given the intense pressures of coursework and exams.

To be clear, I got reasonable grades, but at the end of the experience, none of it amounted to much. It did not help that I could not land a job—despite going for multiple campus interviews. It was clear that I had . . . failed. And the sad thing was that it was not a one-shot failure. It was like a gradual process of being beaten down, month after month, semester after semester—for four years. It was hard not to take it personally. It affected me a lot in terms of my future career choices and what I would do afterwards.

For the longest time this was something that I always saw as a huge failure on my part. I believed then (though I don't necessarily believe now) that I was clearly not cut out to be a scientist or an engineer, and this was a huge blow to my self-image. It was difficult to realize this and even harder to accept it. As one might imagine, it was a sad time, which had a huge impact on my self-esteem and confidence. I did many of the usual things that people do in such situations, which is namely to say that I went into my shell, as it was emotionally wrenching to feel that I was letting down my parents and their expectations of me. There is a whole load of aspects to such situations that can affect a person psychologically and emotionally. In that way, I see those four years as the "dark years." I look at what I went in with, which was so much energy, so much passion for learning and for doing something special—and the experience just beat all that out of me. This is truly sad when you consider how often excitement and energy are devasted through educational structures—the very things that are (in theory) supposed to support creativity and learning.

One of the most important questions a person might ask would be, what were the positives out of this situation? If we're interested in learning, what did you learn or how did you grow? The biggest positive, really, is that I became a much better educator because of these four years because I realized that there are people in my classroom, in every classroom, who have energy and passion, and they fall through the cracks. The fact that they're not doing well is not a measure of what their intellectual or personal worth is, but it is actually the educational system that is holding them back.

There's a similar issue that happens when techies talk about people struggling with technology and say it's "user error." The truth is it's not user error, it is the technology not being designed well. A similar thing happens in education. It's not the learners' fault if they are not doing well—it is our fault. I think my experiences have given me a perspective and a sense of empathy because I could see myself there with every person who was not doing well in my class. It made me a much better educator.

Coming back to the story—there I was in my last year of engineering, without a job, wondering what I would do after I graduated. And, just by chance, I saw a poster for a Masters in Design degree in visual communications at the Indian Institute of Technology in Mumbai (then Bombay). I said "Okay, I'm interested in film, always loved watching and reading about serious cinema. I still love science. I love math. I grew up being inspired by Carl Sagan's *Cosmos* and by Jacob Bronowski's *Ascent of Man*." I knew I still loved this stuff, these ideas, so I thought that, maybe, I can make educational films. Long story short, I applied and got into the visual communications program with the intention of making a career in educational film. The goal was to still keep that love of learning, though not as an active practitioner of science or engineering but rather as a communicator of ideas. That shift transformed my life.

It was there at the Industrial Design Center that I was introduced to the idea of design—something that I did not know much about before, but something I seemed to fit right into. In high school I had a group of friends who shared my interests and we sort of pushed each other along—so that I felt that I belonged in that group. In the four years of engineering, I never felt like I truly belonged. I didn't form that identity. I never became an engineer, internally. But at the Industrial Design Center, I rediscovered a bunch of like-minded people who were all interested in all these different things like typography and visual design, art and literature, psychology and human behavior, and their interconnections.

Everything that I had been doing before, which seemed so haphazard, suddenly came together. It was cool and it resonated with me. Deeply. So even today, I see the world through the lens of design. Everything in the world around me, education, parenting, anything—it's always through the lens of design, and in some ways it was that failure that pushed me in a different direction. Within a couple of weeks, I knew this is where I belonged, which I had never felt in engineering school.

What was also amazing, in hindsight, was how breathtakingly sudden this transformation was—between April of 1988, when I was struggling to figure how what I would do after my engineering degree, to September of the same year, when I had been in design school for a month or so. In just those few months I became a completely different person. For the first time, I found an intellectual home. I found a community. Clearly there was a lot that I didn't know about design, I still had a lot to learn, but that identity clicked right away. In literally a few weeks.

One of the things about being a designer is that at some level you are a dilettante. You dabble in many things, and I've always dabbled in a lot of things. I do photography and I do visual design and I like editing movies and I like to write poetry (however badly) and I love math and biology, and everything in between. What this lens of design has let me do is take all of these disparate interests, activities, and projects and see them not as distractions but as a core part of my identity. I could be whole as a designer in a way that I could never have been as an engineer—at least not as it was done in India.

So now I can write a poem about math, and that's fine. Perfectly fine. In fact, somebody recently emailed me asking me if they could use in their teaching a poem I had written (on a whim) about the Fibonacci sequence. I said, of course, "absolutely go for it." How cool is that.

Furthermore, design is a gift that keeps on giving. Design doesn't live in a vacuum; rather, it lives and breathes in the world and is part of our lives. I bring ideas about design into my teaching and research. I bring a lens of design to the work of reimagining schools and education, to my teaching and to my work with technology and with educators and educational leaders. It is a lens that values the pragmatic even while recognizing the importance of the aesthetic. It allows me to recognize and communicate the fact that functionality and beauty (which have different meanings in different contexts) have to work together in any solutions we come up with for the challenges faced by education.

My experience in the Industrial Design Center took me back to who I really was and also made me realize how lucky I was to have stumbled into that line of work. I wonder about all the people who fall through the cracks of our educational system and what a terrible loss that is, both to the individual and to society at large. Some years ago, I was invited to give a talk at Purdue University. Purdue has an engineering education research center, which was one of the biggest in the nation. I started my talk by saying: "You know, for the longest time, I thought I had failed as an engineer. I'm here today to tell you that you guys failed me. Your field failed me. I didn't fail. You guys never gave me a chance. And who are the other people who you are letting down?" I think I'm a much better educator because of the fact that I failed those four years. If I would have sailed through, I never would have had empathy for the ones who don't get through.

I guess I call this my favorite failure because it is just so salient and profound in my life, and so sudden. One day I was a failed engineer, and suddenly two months later I was a designer. It touched every part of my life and my future. Clearly, I hadn't changed in any dramatic way in those two months, but the context around me had. So, this let me see that when there is failure it is important to understand the context within which that failure occurs and think about how you can change that context into something different in order to move forward. Clearly, nothing significant had changed in me, but what changed, dramatically, was the context, what changed was the framing. Which again, if you think about it, is a designer's way of looking at the world, since a big part of the process of design is how you frame a given problem or situation. And that has been another valuable takeaway from the process of being a failed engineer toward becoming a designer—the idea that how you frame the problem dictates the possibilities and what you are able to do. This matters in education, and it matters in everything, really.

So as a broader takeaway, I think it is important to think about where you feel most comfortable and happy—where you feel most yourself. Maybe that's what you should be trying to do and be, rather than trying to make other people comfortable and happy. If things are not working out, the solution may not be as much about changing yourself as it may be about changing the broader context within which you function.

I know, very well, that this is a privileged point of view. I had the choice to switch my career, I had opportunities early on in life, having the right friends and opportunities that allowed me to indulge in my multiple interests. And when I needed, I could change the context. These options are sadly lacking for many people. Educational opportunities are sadly lacking for too many.

That said, I should also add that it is essential not to take failures personally. Failures are learning experiences. They are not about letting yourself or anyone else down. I think, also, that I share one meta-takeaway from this conversation, this conversation about my favorite failure: which is to say that there is no thing such as a favorite failure. Failure is painful. Period. I sometimes get a bit cranky when I hear this Silicon Valley mantra, about failing forward. Failure is never a goal. It is never fun. I don't ever want to fail, but it happens. But again, life is long and you can look back and say, "Okay, I learned X, Y, and Z from it," but if I could get those four years back, yeah, sure, I would grab it in an instance. There is no reason why I had to fail to find my calling. I'm happy with what I do now, the freedom to play with ideas as being part of my job, and the fact that I can dabble in things that are meaningful to me. And that's been very, very fruitful for me, personally and professionally. A lot of joy comes out of it.

But I am also deeply aware that there are many who do not have these same opportunities and second chances—and we don't hear their stories. So, there should be some humility when we speak of favorite failures, because we never hear from the ones who truly failed—for no inherent fault of theirs, but because the system did them a disservice. It chewed them up and spat them out. Failure, as I said before, is not fun. It's only the lucky few who succeeded despite these failures who can construct a narrative that makes these failures appear meaningful. And that is important to remember. Thus, I guess, I am questioning the very idea of this series, because by its very nature, we hear only from those who, despite some failures along the way, managed to succeed in the end. I worry about all the stories we don't hear, and that, to me, is an imperative to do better, to create systems that prevent such unnecessary, painful failures from happening in the first place.

—Punya Mishra is associate dean of Scholarship & Innovation and professor in the Division of Educational Leadership & Innovation in the Mary Lou Fulton Teachers College at Arizona State University.

Ron: This story raises so many questions, including how to realize hope and navigate disappointments in and beyond what we experience in schools. I think many families see school as a place of hope—they hope this is a way to provide new possibilities and opportunities for their children.

If, however, it becomes an utter disappointment, year after year, after year, it is difficult to maintain hope. Feeling hopeless year after year is a heavy load to carry—brutally heavy, and this story illustrates how this can happen. The thing about the stories in this book, and this one in particular, is that they are hopeful, even though they're sometimes painfully sad and even seemingly devastating. There are still messages about the hopeful possibility of turning that corner and finding meaning, identity, and community. Maintaining that hope and optimism is important, but I think it has to be realistic, it can't be captured in slogans or well-intended pep talks.

It's on us as educators to help establish a hopeful setting . . . one that is actually different from what students may have ever experienced before. This is challenging because there's an understandable lack of trust when there's been so much disappointment.

Students have every right to doubt well-intended educators and think it could actually be worse this year, not better. The onus is on all of us as educators and designers to work towards a more hopeful experience for all students by doing our part to open up new horizons of possibilities.

There are, of course, no guarantees, but maybe we can somehow find hope together.

Laura: As we close this chapter and consider the connection between disappointment and hope as they are connected to failure, we should consider asking:

• What are students hopeful about? What gives them hope?
• How might we help them funnel that hope into something productive?

Second, we can use our conversations about failure and disappointment to develop a shared understanding about failure. We can discuss the interplay between hope and disappointment. We can make disappointment transparent to everyone, making it clear that in order to grow, we will have disappointments.

Disappointment does not have to be shrouded in darkness. We can remind our students that when they feel disappointed it means they had hope for something better, for something different. Holding onto hope means recognizing our disappointing failures as opportunities to understand ourselves better, who we want to become, how we see ourselves, and how we can shape the kind of futures that we all want to live in.

Even in failure there is the hope of learning something new, something unexpected. As you explore your own failures:

- What is still giving you hope?
- What is lighting you up?
- What area of that failure maintains a bright spot?
- Where can we find the kernel of what's possible and use that kernel of what's possible to understand each other better, or our students better?
- How can we design more interesting experiences that allow hope to flourish?
- How can practicing appreciative inquiry (Whitney & Trosten-Bloom, 2010) help us uncover the moments that give us hope?
- How can we use those discovered moments of hope as a kernel to envision what's possible, to understand each other better, or to serve our students better?

Ron: I agree, Laura, it's about finding hope together. It's not like we can give hope to people. But we can work together to maintain hope as educators and work toward building new and more hopeful futures together!

Chapter Five

Perspective

Cynthia Zhou: Original artwork
produced for this book

Mea culpas are sometimes necessary.

—Michael Pryor

Ron: Perspective is a multifaceted concept in the context of failure and learning. Underneath perspectives are all kinds of things, like our confidence, our beliefs, our worldview, and how we sometimes step into a situation.

We may assume that we know the best thing to do in a situation and then, when we take action and we're confronted with another perspective, it can be unsettling. All these different things that are discussed in this book, like the concept of surprise, can knock us off our confident path we've taken. We are surprised by another perspective that's so compelling and undeniable that it requires us to sit with it.

Failure forces us to reexamine the actions from the perspective of someone else and provides us with an opportunity to think about the experience differently. We can continue to try to force our perspective on the situation or we can try to step out of that and think about what failure has to offer us.

We also know from the field of creative studies that plurality of perspectives is a key element of creative experiences (Glăveanu & Beghetto, 2020). We can't think and act in new ways unless we're really willing to engage with different perspectives.

When we make an instructional decision or a classroom management decision and then recognize that it had an unexpected or unintended impact, we must begin wrestling with intent versus impact. Like the curriculum theorist Ted Aoki (2004) has noted, there's always a gap between what we intend or plan and what is experienced by ourselves and others.

Looking back or looking through another lens or perspective can help us recognize where the learning needs to happen or where our learning needs to continue.

Laura: One of the emerging themes in this book is the concept of really looking back at the stories we hold and seeing them through a broader, more pluralistic lens. This perspective in both the temporal and varying viewpoints that we did not initially see. It is an opportunity to examine the assumptions that we are holding that no longer serve us.

Failure can bring up feelings of inadequacy, isolation, and sadness. We therefore may want to shy away from thinking about these moments because they make us feel sad or make us feel like we are incapable of success. How often do we really go back, think about a moment in the classroom that failed, or really try to find the moments that took us on a trajectory toward failure?

In design we often use learning journeys as a way to help students understand what we have learned from their design journeys (Stein Greenberg, 2021). They chart what they learned through the course, what moments pushed their learning, what moments felt stagnant, and how they felt throughout the course of their journey.

Not surprisingly, the moments where students often felt like they were truly learning were also coupled with feelings of inadequacy or frustration. But when you zoom out and examine their entire journey, you realize that their highs and lows, their joys and frustrations have left them with a stronger sense of agency.

Their capacity for *productive struggle* (Hiebert & Grouws, 2007) has increased. Their ability to navigate ambiguity, to recognize that iteration is part of building creative ideas has expanded. The reflective process of identifying their moments of failure coupled with seeing their path to success is grounded in their ability to see their learning not as a series of setbacks but as a process of perspective taking.

Another key element you raised, Ron, is the opportunity to see failure through multiple perspectives. Doing so gives us the opportunity to poke at and play with the idea of whose perspective is being privileged, whose perspective or idea is being challenged or minimized.

When we design lessons, it is easy to create an idea based on our own unique perspective. Sometimes that works out. But when we look back at the failures (and success) we have had through multiple perspectives, we end up seeing missed opportunities to meet another person's needs.

Taking perspective—whether looking back or with multiple lenses—is an invitation to ask whose perspectives need to be heard right now in this lesson plan, this assignment, or this assessment.

For those of us who have been teachers, particularly during our first years of teaching, or whenever we're trying lots of new ideas, this becomes an opportunity to think about how we bring in different perspectives along the way. Not just for one big idea but constantly thinking about multiple perspectives that exist within our classrooms.

Taking in multiple perspectives can help remind us that although failure sometimes feels like isolated action by one person, it is experienced in community. Looking back and looking through different perspectives allows us to uncover moments where we could have listened more to the voices of others.

Ron: As we move forward into this next story, there are a few ideas I invite us to think about in the context of our discussion about perspective. The first is that there's a temporal component. Just as you mentioned, Laura, we can use perspective to look backwards to help us examine something in the past and we can also use perspective to help us look forward before taking action.

When we use perspective to look forward, we might ask ourselves whether we are moving towards success or setbacks. How do we know? What other perspectives might inform our own perspective?

There are multiple perspectives or multiple ways of looking at the failure in the moment itself. Then there's perspective after the moment, and so the idea of engaging with multiple perspectives and recognizing positionality from whose perspective this action is going to lead to positive outcomes and anticipating that there will be multiple perspectives before, during, and after failure is important to recognize.

When we look at failure through these layers of perspective, we see how context, social, cultural, and historical perspectives can really inform different ways of thinking about success and failure. Asking ourselves questions, such as "From whose perspective did this action lead to success or setbacks?" "What can we all learn from understanding different experiences and outcomes of our actions?"

This can be difficult and sometimes painful work, but it can help us all learn how to grow from setbacks and successes. Engaging with different views and experiences is not necessarily about resolving perspectives. Instead, it's about coming together—realizing that any perspective that seems to be fixed and finalized has the capacity to be animated into a new pathway that can lead to deeper understanding and learning.

Exploring even little moments of success and setbacks, through the layers of temporal and positional lenses, can shift us into seeing things with a new and more meaningful perspective.

It may seem terrifying on one hand because the answer of who or what failed may change depending on whose perspective the situation is seen through; but it opens the windows of possibility that can support our learning and understanding of each other—moving us closer to better actions that support positive outcomes in learning. This next story highlights the role perspective plays in learning from setbacks.

PERSPECTIVE: MY FAVORITE FAILURE

By Michael Pryor

It was my second year of teaching and I was still operating under the belief that compliant engagement was the most effective classroom management strategy (do as I say, and THEN we can have a great time). I was a

23-year-old teacher of second-grade students, with a passion for bringing energy and animation into each of my lessons.

Because of my green approach to classroom management, however, I found myself punishing whole groups for the "misbehavior" of a few from time to time. In this instance, I had a select group of students stay at their desks during indoor recess time to write off the board: "I will work hard and not be lazy." They were required to write this 10 times.

A justifiably concerned parent contacted me the next day and requested a conference to discuss the incident. During the conference, I could feel her anger underneath her curt responses that were being delivered under the guise of restraint. I allowed her to speak her mind fully and did not defend myself in the slightest; I knew I had no bearing to do so at that point. She concluded by asking me if I understood why such a punishment would concern her as a mother. I think by this point she was asking this because she knew I was not a parent and was a green 23-year-old teacher. I answered honestly and simply said that such behavior from a teacher would make a parent feel as though their child is not in a place where they are respected, safe, and loved. Of course, I knew that this parent's child WAS all of those things, but I agreed with her that such a consequence displayed quite the contrary.

I realized not only my impact on my students, but the impact of a teacher on a child in general. These kids spend seven hours with us each day, so naturally everything we say or do is going to have a great impact. I let my personal emotions cloud my professional judgment, and this child's excitement for being in my classroom and overall well-being as an eight year old were casualties as a result.

I also learned that in order to form an authentic partnership with parents, we must be able to recognize our opportunity areas. I often see teachers make the mistake of bringing their ego into such conferences, and the line of communication is instantly severed as a result.

I learned that I played a major role in every child's daily life, and no matter how small the action may seem to me, it could be perceived in an entirely different manner through the eyes of my students. I learned that parents sometimes just need to be heard. Defensiveness builds barriers on the lines of communication.

Mea culpas are sometimes necessary.

I also learned that a little noise in the classroom was a good thing, and that if a kid challenges something I say or do, it doesn't necessarily equate to disrespect, as my young, seemingly power-hungry mind initially thought. Not only is an apology sometimes owed to the parents, but also *to the child*!

There was just so much to be taken away from this experience. From parent communication, to the role of the educator as an academic, emotional, mental, and spiritual leader, all of these hats impact the classroom culture. I wasn't just grooming these kids for third grade, I was shaping how they view teachers, and education in general. This is ultimately my favorite failure because although I was incredibly shamefaced, I was able to take a great deal away from this incident, and I still had a shot at redemption as an educator, but more importantly, as a role model and human being.

—*Michael Pryor is the principal of Saint Timothy Catholic School in Chantilly, Virginia.*

Laura: One of the primary questions that emerges from this story is: *Whose perspectives are valued within your classroom?* It reminds us to consider the perspectives of young people we are impacting when designing all aspects of the learning environment (e.g., lesson plans, setting up classrooms, creating discipline plans and student schedules).

Another key insight that this story brings to life is the power that small moments have in challenging our preconceived notions about what our job is supposed to be.

In this story, the parent's perspective about what was happening to their child provided the catalyst for the teacher to reimagine what it means to be a teacher. Taking in this new perspective forever changed how this educator designed learning experiences. When we take in new perspectives, listening to stories that shed a light on how experiences we design affect someone else, it gives us the opportunity to see the long-term impact of our actions.

As educators it is important to ask, "How might the systems, existing practices, or educational ideas we believe negatively impact our students?" Our ability to use perspective to travel to the future and look back and imagine how a lesson, a discipline action, or a conversation might impact a young person is, in a very real way, one of the ways we as educators can shape the future.

Perspective invites us to be futurists by envisioning and examining the long-term impact of an action from the multiplicity of lenses (McBain & Soloman, 2020). As educators, parents, and coaches use this story to engage with new perspectives, we might think about the following questions:

- How did seemingly inconsequential decisions impact others?
- What perspectives do you think young people are likely to leave your classroom with?
- What perspectives do you carry with you when you design your lesson plans?
- Whose perspectives are privileged?
- Whose perspectives need to be understood more?
- Whose perspectives are missing?

Ron: Those are such important questions, Laura, for us all to consider in our work as educators.

These questions align with the above story because they challenge us to think about what we can do to engage with multiple perspectives at the beginning of our design processes, during a lesson, and following a lesson.

Early in our careers, especially as educators there is a lot of pressure to demonstrate what or how a good classroom or disciplinary structure is supposed to look like. Sometimes we draw on perspectives of our past rather than the perspectives of the young people and colleagues before us in the here and now.

What might be different if we had conversations with students about their concerns instead of automatically using our one perspective to make a judgment? Even if such conversations lead to unwanted outcomes, there's powerful data in there too. In this story, the teacher felt shame. Shame is a powerful self-emotion (Tracy & Robins, 2004) that sometimes makes you want to run away from it or hide. But even if the conversation brings up feelings of shame, doubt, or regret, we can use it to see other people more clearly and use it as an opportunity to look inward at ourselves only.

The sometimes-painful reflective acts, as shown in this story, remind us that perspective grants us a chance for redemption. The possibility to

apologize, not only to parents but to students demonstrating even embarrassing or shameful experiences can serve as powerful learning moments
for everyone involved.

When embarking upon a new challenge or idea, there is opportunity to
take in different perspectives. We can ask and build on questions like the
ones you raised, Laura, such as:

- Before acting, how can you try to get the perspectives of those you
  need to learn from before, after, or when you are in the midst of taking
  action? What information can you gather?
- How can you create space for perspectives to be heard and listened to
  before, during, and after acting?
- How can you demonstrate learning by honoring these different perspectives?

Laura: In closing our conversation about this story, it is worth touching
a bit more on the transition from shame to redemption.

Failure hints at shame and prevents people from taking bold action.
Shame spirals, as described by Brene Brown (Brown, 2020), and propels
us into a circle that makes us doubt and mistrust our own actions.

The practice of perspective taking, when rediscovering our failures,
allows us to see the assumptions, beliefs, or biases we're holding about
education and our young people that actually are not serving them or
ourselves anymore.

It gives the redemptive hope we need to design new bold actions using
the lens of hindsight.

Chapter Six

Guilt

Cynthia Zhou: Original artwork
produced for this book

The heroes with power to create tangible change reside in the communities they serve.

—Sophia McGovern

Laura: So many of us don't like to admit our failures to other people because there is an overwhelming sense of guilt that we have let another person down.

In education there is often a profound emotional connection to the young people we are trying to serve. The fear of failure or the risk of failure is coupled with the potential guilt one might feel when we fail to do the best job we can. This often prevents us from taking bold creative risks because there is the real possibility that we might fail and feel saddled with the guilt that we failed a young person.

To help educators and young people release themselves of failure so they can actually take more bold and creative risks, we have to explore our experiences of failure and where the guilt comes from.

Dissecting failure is an opportunity to understand who we are and how we think of ourselves, and it gives us the chance to distinguish between statements like "I failed" versus "this project was a failure."

Dissecting a failure reminds us that the failures—the grittiness of the things we don't achieve—are not necessarily a reflection of our own perseverance or our own imperfection.

Instead, dissecting failure is about recognizing that this project didn't go well this time. No one likes to let other people down. But, as educators, we need to move away from perfectionism if we are ever going to take big, beautiful, bold risks.

Ron: Guilt is one of those emotions that can be so stifling, especially when you're trying to do something new . . . it's an emotional experience you can feel trapped in.

Ruminating on past setbacks and failures and feeling bad about those because you feel that you let yourself or others down can really get in the way of learning from those experiences and trying new things that might help others.

As educators, guilt about a teaching opportunity lost, or a lesson that we didn't feel fully prepared to teach, or even feeling that we failed a student or didn't do enough to help a student learn—all of these experiences can result in stifling feelings of guilt.

These feelings can be a lot to carry, and so guilt is one of those emotions that just kind of lingers and can get in the way of new and creative action. It's such a sticky and powerful emotion that holds us and requires us to learn from it before we can carry forward into new action. Part of it seems to come from feeling accountable, which is important to sit with and learn from. Another part of it seems to come from a deep remorse of wishing we could go back in time and change or erase whatever led up to the failure.

This problematic part of guilt is when we allow it to stop us from taking the actions necessary to work through and learn from our past failures. The danger of this aspect of guilt is it can completely stifle taking beautiful risks of sharing our stories with others, working through them, learning from them, and ultimately carrying the lessons forward.

So if it's a lesson or project that didn't work out and we feel like we let ourselves and others down, then we can carry these lessons forward by reflecting on and sharing these stories. Doing so can help us learn how to recalibrate our expectations, realize that maybe we need to start with some smaller initial steps, or maybe it wasn't the right time, or the right context. This even includes allowing ourselves to shift to some other project that can still benefit others.

If we failed by making a choice or acting in a way that didn't take into consideration the impact it had on others, then we can carry this learning forward by acknowledging it and learning from it by discussing it with those who we impacted and by learning how to infuse empathy and perspectives into future actions we take.

Sharing stories of failure that include feelings of guilt can be a powerful source of learning for those who tell them, hear them, and read them. Learning from and sharing these narratives can help people understand how painful and complicated experiences of letting ourselves and others down can still result in important learning that can transform failure into learning that can be carried forward and benefit our own and others' future actions, learning, and lives.

Laura: The possibility of guilt prevents us from taking bold risks. When we encounter a moment in which we might fail, we time travel to the future envisioning and feeling the potential guilt from that failure. Sometimes we get into analysis paralysis mode (Snowden & Boone, 2007)—being so worried the action that we will take is going to have a negative impact in the future that it prevents us from taking any action at all.

Reflection, which is like time traveling backward and thinking deeply about our moments of failure, can move us from analysis paralysis toward actionable understanding. Conversations with ourselves and with those whom we think we have let down in the past become an opportunity to deeply understand what assumptions or stories we were holding about those moments of failure. These restorative conversations can help us reset our expectations around failure and eradicate the myths we hypothesize about when we attempt to take big, bold risks.

It is in writing and telling of our failure stories where we discover whether the guilt we had or the possible guilt we may feel is grounded in truth.

For young people the failure stories in this book can serve as a time machine to understaning failure. By reading stories about failure we can see what is true, see the possible guilt that could ensue, and use them as constructive constraints for our new ideas.

Ron: I really like that, Laura, because I think there's a lot to be learned by young people and all of us who are trying to take risks and do their part to try to change the world and make it a better place.

Big ambitions come with potentially big setbacks along the way. Also, there are so many well-intended projects, particularly like community-based projects that sometimes carry some negative, unintended consequences.

At the start of community-based projects, there's usually a lot of energy around them, and then for whatever reason, sometimes the energy falls off or ends abruptly. When this happens, instead of making a positive difference, the project can be seen and experienced as a failure that depletes resources, trust, and hope. A lot of feelings of guilt can surround these kinds of failures.

Guilt can be a sign that reconciliation and resolution is needed and, in some cases, this may not be fully possible. But learning can still happen. And the learning that can happen can be a kind of reconciliation by having the conversations about what was intended and what happened and how other people experienced the event or situation, and what was learned from that experience.

This learning can then be carried forward into the planning of new lessons, projects, and experiences, particularly when you're being bold and taking beautiful risks. You might approach those experiences with a recognition of the need to monitor how the project or effort is being experienced and keeping an eye on potentially unintended consequences along the way.

If something does go sideways and it doesn't work out and people are feeling bad about what they were hoping would happen and what happened, then it can be more readily recognized and addressed through conversations and timely adjustments.

This anticipation and commitment to making timely adjustments can be baked into the process, so if something isn't working out it can be learned from and addressed. This doesn't mean that we will never again experience the guilt that comes from setbacks or failing to meet expectations, but that we see those experiences and feelings as actionable and carried forward in our current and future efforts.

GUILT: MY FAVORITE FAILURE

By Sophia McGovern

My dream was to leave the country and alleviate the systemic violence of poverty through international partnerships. I failed and found my calling as a teacher.

In Lyantonde, Uganda, I clung to the back of a motorbike as we made our way to the beneficiaries' new house site and bounced through the orange *fufu*, or dust, that clouded the air. We weaved through other motorbikes carrying up to five people. Pedestrians hauled makeshift cans full of water past schools with children who shouted and waved as they saw a *muzungo*, or "explorer," fly by.

It was 2014, and I was helping to manage a student-run global health nonprofit at Arizona State University that partnered with a grassroots organization in Lyantonde, Uganda. We would fund their housing and sanitation project, while our partner would select the beneficiaries, hire the workers, and oversee the project. My job was to document the construction of the house, help design the next year's budget, and assist with the monitoring and evaluation of past projects. I stayed with the family of our partner's executive director. The executive director's brother, Milton, took me to the villages and was tasked with taking care of their American guest.

We turned off the main dirt road up a footpath that wove through banana plants and maize crops. Children raced up the hill and a floppy-eared, blue-eyed puppy barked playfully behind them. We pulled off at a hut where a mother sat shelling nuts on the ground, and her toddler hid behind her. Milton told me to take pictures and I pulled the camera out of my bag. I barely knew how to use the camera and fumbled with it, while the mother kept her eyes low to the ground. Milton beckoned me to photograph her house and personal belongings. I felt uneasy and out of place as I saw the suit jacket of her departed husband still hanging from between the woven banana-plant strands. What gave me the right as a stranger to do this?

We sat and ate porridge and crispy maize with the family. She was the only worker, and I wondered how much we had taken from her. We walked farther up to the future home site. The plants had been flattened in a rectangular plot with a hole not too far from where the prospective house would be. Milton gestured to the hole as he said, "This is where the pit latrine would have been, but your funds were lacking."

It had been a long year of straining money out of family members, friends, and fellow undergraduates. We had donation drives and events all year, but still we fell short. The dollars we did not raise lay at the bottom of that pit.

We then headed to the previous year's beneficiary family. The father had also died, and the mother was HIV positive and had been sick with opportunistic infections. She was very outspoken and took one look at me, then joked to Milton that I was just like the *muzungos* that had come before. She was proud of her house. Her chickens were doing well, but the roof was leaking, and the rain catchment well was needing service. She was able to work now, but most of her funds would have to go to repairs instead of school uniforms for her children. However, she had a plan.

She marched us up to a hectare of her land she had slashed and burned clear. All she needed was a loan for the seeds. She could have a crop yield seven times greater than the investment and still feed her family. The sun shone down, and she smiled at her dream. However, this money would need to be raised in addition to the funds for the current beneficiaries' pit latrine, and the next beneficiaries' house, latrine, and well. For a while I convinced myself and my team that we could do it, but the partnership dissolved a year later as we fell short yet again.

My friend and I sat on a collapsing futon in our college apartment as we prepared for the final meeting with ICOD's executive director. He was drafting legislation to end FGM and was educating local farmers in permaculture practices and technology use and leading the housing and sanitation projects. After four years of idealism, we finally had to be realistic about what little power we had. We were failing him and the community of Lyantonde.

This realization settled and shifted my life. I was disillusioned with the problematic nature of the global health model but had learned two essential lessons. First, the heroes with power to create tangible change reside in the communities they serve. They use their unique skills to listen to community members, create the space for them to be heard, and advocate for their well-being through consistent dedication. Second, I would work to become one of these leaders.

I returned from Uganda and tried to put the guilt of failure behind me, but the leaky roofs, lifeless pits, and the families we let down still haunt me. To create change, I had to believe in my strengths and listen to community members' needs. I followed my writing skills and found the world of alternative education, a space where opportunity is unequal and hard-won, but possible. Six years later, I am a long way from Lyantonde, but instead, I am home. Today, I teach English Language Arts to scrappy, energetic, and authentic teenagers in a space of challenges and perseverance. A space in which I learn every day and work to build a platform for our youth through true connection and community.

—*Sophia McGovern is pursuing a master's degree in secondary education at Arizona State University and teaches English Language Arts in an alternative high school. She currently runs* little somethings press: a collection of small writings *and serves as an editor for independent presses in Phoenix.*

Ron: This story invites us to think about how we can learn from the guilt of failed endeavors and carry our learning forward into new endeavors and commitments to make a positive difference by being bold and taking those beautiful risks.

The questions that stories like this raise for us as educators, students, community members, parents, coaches, and leaders, include:

- How can we think about and proactively anticipate failures, such that we don't get mired in the ruminations of guilt that stifle our future potential to move forward and support new learning and transformation?
- How can we learn to carry these lessons forward and continue to make a positive difference now and into the future?
- As we're thinking about trying something new, whether it's a new lesson or you're going to take a risk trying something new, how can we think about and anticipate the potential of going sideways?
- How can sharing and discussing stories about failures and guilt associated with those failures serve as opportunities to be inspired, to learn, and to continue to move forward and try to make a positive contribution?

Obviously, you don't have to follow those questions, exactly. However, an opportunity to tell these stories, time travel back to the potentially painful failure, but then recast it as a learning opportunity, provides us with a simple and powerful way to take something that was stuck in the past, bring it forward, and then push it into a more hopeful future.

Laura: I think this story also encourages us to look back and think about moments where our fear of potential guilt led us to *inaction*. We have discussed how guilt from past failures prevents us from taking on actions that might result in failure; but it is equally important to reflect upon how the guilt we projected into the future prevented us from taking any action at all.

Guilt is a powerful motivator. It can stop us from doing terrible things. It also shames us into thinking that inaction is safer than taking necessary action. How can thinking about moments of inaction help us understand and get us closer to our own fear of failure?

- Think about a time when you chose not to take a risk because you dreaded letting another person or your community down. What was the result of that inaction?

Also, because guilt is a powerful motivator, it can also force us to reflect on failures that really did have a negative impact.

Failure and the guilt surrounding it may feel like an immovable boulder, but opening ourselves to those we think we have hurt and reflecting together on the impact of that failure can give us the opportunity to release the guilt that we might have been feeling around that past failure and allow us to move forward.

- Think about a time when you feel like a mistake you made negatively impacted someone else. What happened? How might you connect with this person to understand the impact of your actions?

As daunting as this question might be, it is also an opportunity to reconnect and reconcile the stories you hold about those failures. If connecting with a person is impossible, writing about these moments also provides an opportunity to help understand your own failure journey and its impacts on others.

Chapter Seven

Surprise

Cynthia Zhou: Original artwork
produced for this book

The following uncertainties became the structure from which my growth would occur.

—Garrett J. Jaeger

Laura: Part of the mystery behind failure is this opportunity to surprise yourself. The surprise lies in the spectrum between what could be a success and what could be a failure. When we put ourselves in new, possibly risky moments, there is a high level of uncertainty and ambiguity about how an idea, project, or lesson will go.

We can do countless hours of planning, testing, and discussing, but in the end we often have very little control about how an idea or lesson will be received in the world. When it goes well there is a surprising moment of relief, and if it goes poorly there is a surprising sinking feeling of regret.

Failure gives the opportunity to surprise ourselves in what we can do or who we are becoming. As we grow, we become accustomed to removing or eradicating surprise from life because it can feel chaotic or disruptive; *but what if we could see failure as pivotal moments in our lives to surprise ourselves?*

Surprise is the gift that failure affords us because it unfolds in the moment often with little notice or anticipation.

Ron: Yes. Failure asks for our willingness to be surprised and almost anticipate it. In a world where we plan for everything, including making lesson plans, there is a large amount of anticipation. We anticipate how it might go. Sometimes we are relieved. Other times we might regret the outcome. But in every case, there is some level of surprise.

Moments of surprise and how we respond to them serve as defining moments (see Beghetto, 2017). We can have all kinds of slogans on our classroom walls that encourage us to soar big, design-defining moments, but failure gives us the chance to see how we react in the moment of surprise. This is a big part of what this book is about.

The stories in this book invite us to ask ourselves the kinds of questions that can lead to new thought, action, and learning, such as:

* What do you do with those moments that just are completely different from what you plan for or expected?
* How are these moments framed as a failure versus a success?
* How can we retrospectively rethink those moments as our favorite failures?
* So how do we prepare ourselves for being surprised and learn how to navigate those moments better?

Sometimes these moments are jarring, but even then, they still give us a chance to reflect on what we envisioned and what really happened. Surprise is a powerful signal that what we are doing is a new opportunity for learning or an opportunity to do something creative.

The next story does a nice job of highlighting how surprise can sometimes be uncomfortable, awkward, and even isolating. Surprise can make us feel unprepared or naive, but in reality, these moments can be important moments of learning in our lives.

Laura: In the upcoming story, Garrett (the author) puts forth the idea that an important meeting in his academic journey was surprising and disappointing. He had a history in academia and felt like he was approaching the situation with kindness and a free lunch.

He assumed what he had envisioned would go as planned, but within moments he felt this pang of surprise; he felt like an outsider and his sense of belonging in that space was disrupted.

As educators, how do we flip the script of what is surprising versus unsurprising? We have young people who may feel like they don't belong, who feel like their words do not matter, so it's not surprising that they don't show up, don't take risks, or don't share their ideas more boldly. They might have experienced surprising moments that have taught them it is unsafe to take risks.

How can we create classrooms where a sense of belonging does not feel like a surprise? How can we start behaving in ways that surprise our students and others with trust, with care and the sometimes-surprising ideas that they matter to them?

There have been so many moments in our lives where we've been taught how things are going to play out. We have the scripts in our heads. And these scripts get reinforced when we experience an unsurprising moment of failure, lack of trust, aggression, or disappointment.

How can we work with our young people to rewrite those scripts to transform moments where they thought they might feel a lack of trust or belonging into a cadre of moments where trust, kindness, care, belonging, and authenticity is the unsurprising norm?

Students should not feel like trust, or a sense of belonging, is a surprising trait in schools. How can we create schools where it is unsurprising that all students thrive, where all students feel a sense of belonging, and that all students feel trust?

SURPRISE: MY FAVORITE FAILURE

By Garrett J. Jaeger

There are times when our weaknesses are shown to us in such a way that sends ripples through our identity and the plans we make around it. One failed meeting reframed a decade of work, and it shoved me into the deep end of a pool into which I had just begun to wade.

This story of failure is about a long climb from rural America to the halls of a prestigious university, and how the earth seemingly disappeared beneath my feet on the last step of that particular climb.

Shortly after completing a graduate school program, I packed a tiny car with my belongings and golden retriever, as I sought a greater challenge elsewhere. Along the way, I made a lot of stops and even more assumptions; each exposing ambition and naivete.

Shedding light on weakness was a wise move then, and it continues to be so to this day. That is not to say that such exposure does not invite failure and even pain.

This story of failure unfolds inside a research lab that investigated, among other things, how infants evaluate whether the encouragement of a caregiver was worth crawling over seemingly uncertain ground. I had not conducted psychological research in a few years, and, in fact, my prior graduate program presented science as a dubious exercise in confirmation bias.

In many ways, I was taking risks vis-á-vis my relocation and these intellectual pursuits. At the time, I could not see the parallel between the emotional precipice before me and the cliff children would cross during studies in this prospective lab.

After a series of delayed email responses between a prospective mentor and me, we finally agreed to meet for a chat about my joining his research lab. This agreement was ultimately agreed upon after my offer (i.e., bribe) to bring food so as to free up the lunchtime hour for this faculty member. After arriving at the lounge of the research lab, I sat speaking with doctoral student lab members about research while waiting for their boss.

As the wait grew longer, and the conversations became increasingly sparse, the other attendee of the proposed meeting finally entered the lounge long enough to tell the lab manager that some kid who wanted to join the lab was going to stop by, so tell him to come back another time. As the literal head of the figurative Head of the lab turned to disappear behind the door from which it had emerged, I said, "Hello, would you at least have time to walk me back to the stairs?"

The gentleman was visibly embarrassed and flustered, as was I. After accepting his offer to chat for the remaining ten minutes of the lunch hour, the dialogue was superficial and one-sided, with my side never being expressed. However, I did leave with twice the amount of lunch I had anticipated, and frankly, could even afford.

My expectations were grounded, and my ambition took a substantial hit that day. On most other days, I was confident in my ability to express myself and engage in meaningful intellectual dialogue. But, on this day, neither me nor my ideas were earnestly invited to the kid-sized table placed in that children's observation room. I left that day wondering how to even begin to reevaluate my life's plans to enter academia after having been dismissed in such a way. But first, a new plan: ration those two sandwiches until I could afford groceries again.

I learned a lot that day about what it felt like to be on the outside of a community in which I assumed to be. There appeared to be an intellectual strata to which I was either naive, unprepared, or unadaptable. I visited many other university faculty seeking mentorship, each advising me to attain proper training before entertaining such ambitions. And that is what I did . . . over the next many years.

That one day, which held both the highest and lowest moments of my aspirations, pushed me to venture further into an unknown world. This time though, such steps honored my not knowing, rather than me assuming I would be seen.

The following uncertainties became the structure from which my growth would occur. Not so ironically, this failure, and how I felt afterward, has informed the theoretical foundation from which my academic career has been built: how does uncertainty motivate us to explore new approaches?

I now play my own game, among others who play theirs. And now, when I am offered a chance to share a sandwich, I stay awhile and help that player see through their game.

—Garrett J. Jaeger, PhD, is a research specialist at the LEGO Foundation in Billund, Denmark. His research focuses on mapping exploratory behaviors to better understand links between play and creativity.

Ron: After having read through the story and thinking about some of the things we talked about prior to this story, the idea of welcoming unwelcome surprises is a powerful idea for anyone who is an educator, parent, coach, or designer of learning environments.

We can't always imagine how students are necessarily going to react or think. We find ourselves designing something that we think will be a welcome experience, but we can be quite surprised when we find out that our students did not experience a lesson or activity in the way we imagined. This highlights how a seemingly well-intended act can be experienced as an unwelcome surprise by students.

Surprise in this case seems to be rooted in the idea that something is welcome or unwelcomed. It comes with intentions, anticipation, and expectations that serve as unchecked assumptions. We can start to check these assumptions by asking ourselves questions like,

- How might we design learning experiences that ensure students have a voice and can talk about what is a welcoming and unwelcome surprise?
- How can we learn from those moments?
- How can we explore welcoming and unwelcome surprises with our students?
- How can we minimize the unwelcome surprises and then learn how to actually navigate them when they do occur in a productive way?

It's also important to have conversations with students and to design *welcomed surprises* in our schools and classrooms. Even though welcomed surprises still involve uncertainty, which can initially feel uncomfortable, those welcome surprises are where learning and growth can take place. We don't want classrooms that are completely unsurprising because they become boring and overstructured.

Classrooms that don't entertain surprises leave no room for new thought. Everything is predetermined, so the learning is overly constrained. Classrooms like this result in a game of "intellectual hide and seek" (Beghetto, 2013) where the goal is to uncover what's already known.

The balance lies in creating unsurprising spaces where risk is supported and trust is guaranteed and welcoming the kinds of surprising experiences where everyone, including the teacher, can learn and grow.

Laura: This story reminds me that there are certain things in classrooms that we don't want to be surprising. It should be unsurprising for a student to feel trusted. It should be unsurprising for a student to have a voice and be heard in the classroom. It should be unsurprising for students to have their teachers believe in them and respect who they are.

A culturally responsive teacher (Gay, 2002) should feel unsurprising in schools and classrooms. Norms, systems, and structures that hold that the pluralistic view (Escobar, 2018) that there are multiple ways of thinking and being should be unsurprising to students.

Welcomed surprises should be central to what students are doing when they are learning, exploring, and building new ideas and projects.

We often hear stories from young people about the one teacher who believed in their capacity for greatness. At the core of these stories is the idea that this one teacher acted in a way that was surprising to the young person. It was a welcomed surprise.

How can we ensure that these kinds of surprising moments become unsurprising moments in schools and classrooms? And, at the same time, design experiences where students are surprising themselves by what they can do and who they are becoming?

Here are some questions to consider as we all work toward establishing more welcomed surprises in our schools and classrooms:

- What should be an unsurprising truth or norm in your classroom that will make it safe for all students to take risks or feel a sense of belonging?
- How might we cultivate moments where students will surprise themselves with the failures that they undertake?
- How can we create moments of failure where students are not risking their sense of themselves or their own identity in pursuit of a grade or outdated curriculum?
- How can create experiences where a culture of belonging is flourishing?
- How can you surprise yourself through new experiences and ways of thinking?

Chapter Eight

Embarrassment

Cynthia Zhou: Original artwork
produced for this book

The failure taught me little about the immediate situation and served little purpose in that moment, but it did teach me that it's okay to fail and that the pain of failing soon fades.

—Wendy Ross

Ron: Embarrassment is one of those double-whammy emotions that we can experience when we fail. This is because the setbacks or failures happen publicly, so it carries that extra intensity of failing in front of others. This is the kind of failure that many of us fear most, because we don't want to make fools of ourselves, particularly when we're doing something that might be important or that we thought we could do successfully.

When it all falls apart, in front of other people, it's a difficult experience to overcome. It's one of those experiences that we don't want to replay or, worse yet, we can't stop replaying in our minds. It can even grow into the more intense and stifling experience of shame (Tracy & Robins, 2004). In such moments, we just want to disappear (Scheff, 2003).

This experience is something I've explored in my own work (Beghetto, 2013; Beghetto & Dilley, 2016). Specifically, how experiencing embarrassment and shame can profoundly stifle creative expression and put our aspirations on indefinite hold. When we experience this, what I've called *creative mortification*, we stop pursuing that creative aspiration because trying again seems both too painful and even impossible.

So, embarrassment is one of those experiences that doesn't just quickly resolve itself and thereby makes it difficult or too painful for us to think about or even identify what was learned from that moment. Cliches, like time heals all, seem so hollow and empty because some embarrassments feel like no amount of time will heal them.

That said, I do believe sharing stories of favorite failures can provide a different perspective and maybe help us learn through embarrassing moments. Sometimes we can find a moment of humor in our own embarrassments when sharing them with others.

At the very least, connecting with and empathizing with what other people might be experiencing can help us realize shame and embarrassment. These moments can also sometimes help us realize how the embarrassing experience has helped to shape who we are now.

I think there is real potential and power in sharing favorite failure stories, even those that are somewhat painful or embarrassing to tell, because they can still carry with them lessons that can help support our own and others' learning and growth.

That's the whole point of this kind of project. It represents the beautiful risk of sharing those stories with others with the hope that they can contribute to others. Sharing these stories of failures provides us all with new ideas and perspectives on how to navigate learning and creativity in our own lives.

Laura: The next story highlights and reminds us that there are moments in our lives where we literally just didn't do something well and, in particular, we didn't do something well in public.

This public failure, this embarrassment, is literally a full-body experience. It takes over your whole body, your face might go red, your stomach might drop, your limbs feel shaky, all because you realize you just made a mistake.

In schools, public embarrassment can feel even worse because from the moment we enter kindergarten we are taught and socialized to be always in control.

Students are expected to have the idea of school figured out. Students and sometimes teachers are rewarded when students sit quietly in rows, remain quiet and act in accordance to what is expected of them. But when things go off script and a classroom or a student behaves differently than what is expected, there is both internal and external possibility of embarrassment.

Simple mistakes made by a young person can crescendo into a yearlong journey of embarrassment. We feel embarrassed and sometimes others start feeling embarrassed for us because they, too, have experienced public embarrassment.

However, when we acknowledge these moments of public embarrassment with others, we are able to move on, laugh, and look back knowing they are merely a part of being human. When we share these moments with others, we let some of the air out, and the seriousness that can show up as shame can be released.

If we can understand that embarrassment is just part of life, it's part of growing, it's part of being human, it might allow us to feel a bit more connected to each other and be more honest about the mistakes we make.

Ron: Yes, and it is often the case, in this place we call school, that only positive emotions are welcome. So, feeling anger or frustration or embarrassment usually is not allowed, even though, like you said, we can all remember feeling the embarrassment for another person.

I think being able to name that and talk about it, without fear of doing so, can become part of the educational process. In this way, even negative emotions can be welcome in schools and classrooms. When we share these kinds of stories, we can do just that.

The other thing you mentioned, which is important to keep in mind as we move into this next story, is that the full-body, visceral experience that we can have when we experience embarrassment, when we have a public setback, it is also a shared experience. Other people feel it too!

This story also highlights that if you fail something once and then you go back later and try to do it again, and you fail again, even more spectacularly and more publicly, then you can have this deep, visceral embarrassing wave of emotions so much so that you feel completely alone in the moment (even though you are not).

EMBARRASSMENT: MY FAVORITE FAILURE

By Wendy Ross

There are three broad types of failure I have encountered in my life.

The first is when failure is a built-in part of progression. We often see this sort of failure in sport. For example, I like to weight train. It is unsafe to lift heavy weights without knowing what to do when it goes wrong, so the training for the larger lifts is interwoven with training to fail those lifts.

You lift only as heavy as you know how to fail safely so there is a necessary intimacy and acceptance of failure: *This is failure as progress*.

Second is the failure that comes from the trial-and-error explorations of potential solutions that I encounter and evidence as part of my research into problem-solving. I watch participants in the psychology labs move ever closer to a solution bit by bit and incrementally while encountering multiple failures. *This is failure as discovery*. It is a Thomas Edison approach to failure: "I haven't failed, I have just found 10,000 ways that don't work."

The third is what I like to call a "sucky" failure. It doesn't fit easily into the cultural narrative that recasts failures as learning opportunities. These failures are unexpected and unfair. No immediate and clear good comes out of these failures. There is no progression. It just sucks. It hurts and it takes time to get over it. Life is full of these sorts of failures, which are rarely mentioned because we are ashamed of them. My favorite failure is one of those.

In the United Kingdom we can take our driving test at age 17. I lived in the countryside and my parents were fed up with being taxi drivers. For my seventeenth birthday, I received an intensive course of lessons that guaranteed you would pass your test. I failed spectacularly; the school returned my parents' money rather than waste more time teaching me.

I got good at cycling. Then when I was pregnant with my second child, my husband bought me driving lessons, reasoning that I could not be as bad ten years later. And he was right. I was not as bad. Indeed, I almost passed the first time I took the test apart from driving a little too fast. That was a "learn from" failure. The next test, I buckled up and drove perfectly.

I knew I had done well as we turned down the road into the test center and the instructor had a clean sheet and a smile on his face. As we pulled into the parking lot, he turned to me: "I am very pleased to inform you . . ."

I don't know what happened next.

There was a slight incline to enter the parking lot, and I think I probably took it a little too fast. Whatever the reason, the parking wasn't as smooth as the rest of the drive. In fact, I managed to drive the car straight into the wall of the test center. Not only that, but it hit right next to the window of the room where the examiners take their break.

The window was flung open and people poured out of the building to see what was happening. And I, seven months pregnant, lost the plot, stepped out of the car and threw a toddler-style temper tantrum (foot stamping and all) in front of them. My husband, who was waiting for me with our actual toddler, swiftly took me home. Sobbing. The negative emotions I encountered at that stage were pretty overwhelming.

I went for another test a week later and passed. It was humiliating returning to the site not only of the failure but my epic tantrum. I learned nothing about driving from the failure itself (I did not need to enact the accident to know crashing into the wall of the test center was not a great idea). Sucky failures sometimes hurt most because there is no obvious learning—just a great mess of horrible feelings.

Then several years later, my preteen son came home after failing at a school test he expected to pass. I told him the story of my failure and my poor behavior, and in the telling it turned from a shameful secret into a cheery anecdote.

This failure is a favorite because it is so ridiculous. To fail your driving test by driving into the test center is a pretty unusual experience. The failure taught me little about the immediate situation and served little purpose in that moment, but it did teach me that it's okay to fail and that the pain of failing soon fades.

Life would be a little less fun if we did everything perfectly; I wouldn't be the same person I am now if I hadn't encountered that failure. I would find it a little harder to laugh at myself. To take risks. I would also find it harder to appreciate that "sucky" failures become part of the tapestry of our life.

Failures don't have to lead to success or personal growth but they are part and parcel of what makes you, and for that reason they are priceless.

—Wendy Ross is a researcher based in the United Kingdom. Her research area is creativity and problem-solving, and she uses quantitative and qualitative methods to track thinking. She has failed many times and hopes to fail a lot more!

Laura: This story serves as a call to action for all of us. I have had many moments of embarrassment, where I felt completely out of my element— my stomach crashed, I was sweating, and my face was flushed.

Anyone who has watched someone else make a mistake, a public mistake, is often overwhelmed with the cringe-worthy knowledge of how this person potentially could be feeling right now because we've experienced these feelings ourselves.

As we explore public failures, how do we welcome embarrassment and see it as an opportunity to connect with others? How can we see these moments of embarrassment as vehicles toward mutual vulnerability where this is a reciprocal welcoming of appreciation?

We've all experienced embarrassment. How do we not brush it aside but use it to connect more deeply with people around us?

Embarrassment means we feel we did something wrong, which also means we might have experienced a moment of creative courage. How do we see moments of embarrassment as acts of creative courage?

Embarrassment is felt internally but witnessed externally; so, what is our collective responsibility in being with others through these moments?

What is the ask of the people in the community to be with that person in this moment of embarrassment? Can we share another moment of our own embarrassment? Can we say "wow that must have really hurt"? How can we show up better for each other?

When our young people are experiencing these moments of embarrassment, how can we ensure that they feel less alone in these moments?

Ron: Such great questions, Laura! These questions make me think about the very beginning of any kind of learning experience. Perhaps it is the start of a school year or starting a workshop or just starting a new day, we have an opportunity to anticipate that there likely will be setbacks and failures and maybe even embarrassing failures as we learn together.

So, what if we anticipate it? What if we set the expectations around what we might do to support each other during those moments? Because, if we don't acknowledge this in advance, then I think it's difficult to try to do it only when it happens. It is difficult to do in the moment, because you don't want to further embarrass somebody.

So rather than being silent in that moment we can reach out. Remaining silent during moments of embarrassment makes those moments painfully uncomfortable and alienating. People feel isolated from each other, even though they are sharing in the embarrassment.

What if we have these conversations and share these stories as a way of proactively anticipating embarrassing moments? So, when it does happen, we can step into the moment right there and say "I'm really struggling here" or we can show our support to others in ways that were discussed in advance?

What if we establish, in whatever group, team, class some agreed-upon ways where people can step in and even share their own stories of similar events, such as, "This reminds me of an experience I've had . . ."

And so maybe there can be that community and support in place because it is established in advance.

Laura: Yes, I agree, anticipating moments of embarrassment can be a design intention. This story and this conversation raise several questions for all of us to reflect on, including:

- As educators and designers, how can we intentionally design moments of challenge, where embarrassment is not necessarily seen as a negative, but as part of the learning process?
- What might happen when someone makes a mistake or feels embarrassed; they recognize it as part of the actual learning process?
- How can community members hold a space for those going through those moments of embarrassment and see that the public moments of embarrassment are opportunities to acknowledge creative courage?

Chapter Nine

Honesty

Cynthia Zhou: Original artwork
produced for this book

*Radical honesty meant rejecting the idea that I had to be everything for
everyone—always, and forever. And that I had to do it well and joyfully.*

—Elyse Burden

Ron: When I think of what honesty means, in relation to failure and
learning from failure, what comes to mind for me is that there's such
pressure to avoid mistakes in schools and classrooms. When we make
mistakes it's hard to be honest about them. I think that goes for both
students and educators.

It's difficult, then, to be honest about failures and setbacks and to share
stories about them. But, what would it look like if students could honestly
say, "I didn't understand this . . ." or teachers could say, "I really didn't
know what to say to a student who surprised me with an unexpected question" or educational leaders could say, "we are facing a really difficult
challenge as a school and I'm not sure how we should move forward"?

So maybe it's about being honest about what we don't know. What if we took time to honestly listen and tried to understand what our students are experiencing when we don't know where their questions are coming from, rather than gently redirecting or quickly dismissing them. What I call, "killing ideas softly" (Beghetto, 2013).

What if we were to be honest about that and say, "I really don't know, but I am willing to learn"?

What if we started with being honest with ourselves about our own not knowing? Would that help us be more honest about mistakes we make and the failures that we've had? Will that allow us to learn from them (rather than pretend like they never happened)?

So, again, what if we started out by being honest about what we don't know; then maybe it will build the courage to be more honest with ourselves and others when we are making mistakes and when we need assistance, and in turn be more honest in how we listen and support others who need help, have made mistakes, and are trying to learn from those mistakes.

Laura: As a former classroom teacher, I remember believing that I had to know the right answer to every question a student asked. One of the hardest challenges in education and which manifests in the systems employed in classrooms is the idea that failure should not be celebrated.

We applaud high scores, perfect attendance, and orderly and sometimes quiet classrooms. But if we are being honest, learning is about discovering and building new skills and knowledge, which means that failure is an inevitable part of the learning process.

Students' fear of not being accepted is manifested through peer pressure, which means they might not share an imperfect idea or answer, because it doesn't feel good to not know something or not to do well at something when others around you are excelling.

Equally interesting is that peer pressure to fit in also may manifest in students trying not to be successful. There is a spectrum that exists in classrooms. A student does not want to be perceived as too smart and successful nor too unsuccessful or perceived a failure.

This "middleness" and lack of honesty results in varying degrees of behavior. Some students become disruptive because the fear of failure is harder to deal with than admitting they might need help. Other students hide their brilliance, shying away from moments where the fear of failing to fit in becomes greater than their interest in learning.

How do we create a culture where our students can be honest about the struggles they are facing in and outside of school? How can we create a culture where an authentic "I don't know" is an acceptable response by both students and teachers?

I think part of the answer lies in our ability as educators to be honest with ourselves and our students when we know we are failing. To accept failure, to create a culture where failure can be celebrated, we must begin to be honest about the moment(s) that we are failing.

This means not brushing aside moments with "I've got this" to having conversations with others that begin with "I don't know how to teach this; I don't know how to reach this young person." I have worked with countless educators who know how to share these vulnerabilities with their students and others, but these same teachers still exist in a system where there is pressure to succeed on all fronts.

Some more experienced teachers who have excelled for the past 15 years may be afraid to try new pedagogy or new curriculum because the inevitability of failure is real for the first time in a long time. New teachers feel pressure to get their contract renewed; they aim for perfectionism or experience burnout because they do not want to fail.

So educators also swim through this spectrum between being perceived as a failure to being perceived as overly successful. We put success and failure on a spectrum where success means good, and failure means bad. But learning does not exist in these moments of polarity—learning happens in the squishy middle where one lesson feels like a win and the next feels like a loss.

If we are going to help our students get better at understanding and embracing failure, we have to be transparent about our own failures. It is this radical honesty the upcoming story evokes and provides us an opportunity to be honest about how we are thriving and how we are struggling, really.

Ron: There's so much to unpack in what you said and this upcoming story. Something that jumped out at me when you were talking is this idea of being honest with others and being honest with ourselves. There is an interesting tension when we hit that point where we feel like we have failed, or we can't be successful.

How can we be honest about that moment? I also think there's a lot of times that we all start recognizing that something is not working out but keep doing the same behavior. How can we be honest with our struggles before it turns into a failure?

This raises so many additional questions, such as: What would it be like if a student was to share what they did not understand early instead of waiting until the end of semester and receiving a failing grade? Or a teacher was able to be honest in early weeks of their semester they were starting to burn out or they really did not know how to connect with this young person or teach a particular lesson? Or if an administrator facing a big challenge was to seek assistance from colleagues, their staff and community before an ensuing challenge turned into a political disaster?

Being honest brings up issues of competence. To be honest with ourselves brings the fear that others might see us as being incompetent. And this fear of incompetence runs through the whole system.

Asking for help when we need it is actually a sign of competence. Still, this is difficult to do and therefore it's not surprising when students are not honest with themselves or others when they feel like they can't be successful, but they could be, if they could just ask for help.

It also raises an important question about social competence. What if a new student doesn't know how to talk to a group of well-established friends? They might fear approaching a group of students in the lunchroom because they fear feeling awkward or rejected. How might they be honest with themselves and with others so they can get the help they need? And, of course, there are no guarantees that it will work out.

So, there is a tension between being honest about what is needed and not being honest because of the perceived risk of incompetence or rejection. The irony is, though, to get competent, we need to ask for help when we need it.

To get to the next level whether it's academics or teaching or leadership or life in general, how can schools and classrooms create spaces where people feel supported in taking the risk of being honest and asking for help? And how do we as educators, parents, coaches, and leaders model taking those risks?

As we think about this concept of failure, how are we able to see the signs of our own struggle and be honest when it's time to ask for help?

And when we do ask for help, what are the hazards or benefits of doing that, and what are the hazards of not asking for help when we need it?

Laura: Part of what the stories in this book are helping us to do is to reframe what success is or what success looks like. One of the challenges connected to failure within K–12 education across the United States is its deep connection to how success is connected to dominant culture.

Outdated and harmful racial and cultural norms permeate across K–12 schools, and they perpetuate what success is supposed to look like, which then exacerbates and makes it almost impossible for non-dominant groups to succeed. This is particularly true for Black, Indigenous, and Students of Color in our schools. Success and failure are often viewed in terms of race and cultural norms. And so, in our quest to understand honesty and its connection to failure in schools, we need to understand and gain an awareness of how our own implicit biases perpetuate a singular view of behavior, norms, and success.

How do cultural norms that stem from the dominant narrative prevent us from being honest about what is deemed a failure or a mistake and what is lauded a success?

So when we think about honesty and failure, it is not just acknowledging how we are being honest with ourselves but also how the culture in the classroom exacerbates failure and sets up a powerful segment of our young people to fail just by nature of their own skin color.

Honesty also means acknowledging and dismantling structures of systems that preordain young people to fail. The more that we operate within a system that views our young students as failures, the more we are complicit in perpetuating the belief that failure is connected to race and identity and experience rather than being part of the productive struggle of learning.

How are the systems, practices, and beliefs making students feel like failures when they walk through the front door of school? How are lessons structured and which are privileged that eradicate a sense of belonging?

How can we open ourselves up to a pluralistic definition of success and failure—suggesting that there are multiple ways of knowing, being, and thinking rooted in specific places and communities (Escobar, 2018)? The next story highlights how our understanding and history with failure are rooted to our own identities.

HONESTY: MY FAVORITE FAILURE

By Elyse Burden

"What's my superpower? I'm built like an ox. It seems like I can carry an endless amount of weight." That was me, speaking to a group of colleagues during an icebreaker at SXSWedu [South by South West Education conference] in March 2017.

A nervous breakdown two years later would tell a different story. By that time, Real World Scholars (the organization I cofounded and run) was supporting roughly 250 classroom-businesses around the country. We had started another multi-million-dollar project—one that I was less interested in but would take much of my time and mental energy.

And, we were knee deep in a third project that my cofounder was adamant that we pursue, because while we didn't have the additional staff or resources to support it—we had a "unique opportunity to bring it to life" . . . or something.

My home life was equally chaotic. As the recent guardian of my niece and nephew (then age 12 and 9, respectively), I tried to fuse my 70-hour workweek startup lifestyle with my new insta-parent role—which meant that even on days that were mapped out from 4 a.m. to 11 p.m., I still regularly forgot a kid at school or dropped the ball on an important email because my brain was mashed potatoes.

At the time of said breakdown, no amount of coffee, internal pep talks, and lucky breaks could hide the fact that I was burnt out. As it turned out, an ox I was not.

It took longer to detect than it should have. Self-awareness is a challenge when you combine an aspirational attitude with a too-fast, too-furious pace. We had done this at Real World Scholars, from the beginning and throughout our quick expansion. But this nose-to-the-grindstone approach had its consequences, blind spots turned almost-fatal failures.

When I met my cofounder, John, in 2013, we asked, "how might we use his resources to support real world student entrepreneurship?" Both creatives, we'd experienced the entrepreneurial learning process firsthand and knew how expansive it could be for young people. And while there were barriers, there were also educators all around the country looking for a way to give their students these experiences. (We'd talked to hundreds of them, personally.) It was our job to remove what was standing in their way.

Neither of us educators, we came humble but hungry. We were relentless about the problem and developed a dozen terrible ideas in attempts to solve it. We committed ourselves to championing teachers and their needs, knowing they were linchpins to the whole operation. After 18 months of research and development, we landed on a solution that would allow any classroom to run a business and integrate entrepreneurship into the learning experience. We launched the EdCorps program.

That first year was wild. We started with ten brave teachers around the country, all starting businesses in their classrooms. We worked closely with these teachers. I helped them build e-commerce websites and navigate district rules, secure farmer's market permits, and field media inquiries.

We filled in every possible gap—even when that meant pulling over at a truck stop in Bakersfield at 11 p.m. to troubleshoot last-minute details before a classroom's big launch. It went really well, for what it's worth.

And while often sloppy and patchwork, the experience was powerful for students. We grew fast—from 10 classes to 250 in one year. We onboarded anyone willing to give it a try—with the ongoing promise that "we" would walk them through the process to make it work. Even as our teacher support transitioned to our small (but mighty) team, more visibility meant more opportunities, more school districts and potential partners, more invitations to facilitate workshops, more seats at more tables.

In a world that assumes perpetual growth, we said "yes" over and over again. And as the scope of work grew, our staff didn't, and I was left to upskill in real time to make good on our commitments and the most of our opportunities.

I learned about strategic planning, content writing, team management, graphic design, human resources, grant writing, contracts, partnerships, and fundraising—mostly through extensive googling, incredible mentors, and messy mistakes.

And it was easy to overlook this soul-sucking pace—because such is the commonly accepted story of the entrepreneur. We glorify long hours and an undeterred commitment to the cause, no matter the cost. I was the Jill of All Trades who could #RiseandGrind, overcoming every obstacle necessary to get everything done.

But navigating these spaces—professional, sometimes corporate, and mostly white—often left me feeling performative and ill-equipped. Imposter syndrome is a drag that way. Ox-like strength and resilience—I thought—were my superpowers. I also thought they could sustain both me and the work, despite lots of warning signs to the contrary.

Alas, the pace and pressure were unsustainable and I started to crack. Projects stalled. The work weakened, silly mistakes occurred, important balls dropped. I became less present, lower functioning, and, at a certain point, downright inoperable. I found myself in a mental health crisis that had me swinging through manic episodes as my brain tried to rise to the challenge, despite being exhausted and empty. My body was in a similar state of distress, having lost my ability to eat and sleep normally. My systems were in a full state of rebellion.

One thing became clear. I was not okay, I hadn't been okay, and I didn't know that until it was too late. Undoing the damage done—both to my human being and to our team—required replacing radical resilience with radical honesty.

This meant getting honest, first with myself, then with the people around me. It meant admitting I was overwhelmed and unwell, and that while I could do many things, I couldn't continue doing everything.

It meant pumping the breaks on ongoing projects and walking away from new and exciting ones that I knew weren't feasible—no matter how attractive. It meant acknowledging my whole humanity and naming that my new role as a de facto mother was the hardest thing I'd ever done and had impacted my ability to do the work. Radical honesty meant rejecting the idea that I had to be everything for everyone—always, and forever. And that I had to do it well and joyfully.

It sounds so simple, but in a world that values output, you have to unlearn the idea that you're a machine built for productivity and service to others. And as a woman of color—as is the case with those on other rungs of the social ladder that require you to fight for the space you take up—the world doesn't offer much permission to rest or accept mediocrity. Zora Neale Hurston was right when she said, "If you're silent about your pain, they will kill you and say you enjoyed it." Unchecked success didn't kill me, but the silence and self-deception I traded for it along the way almost did.

It's easier on this side—being honest about my humanity. I'm not an ox, static and stoic in my strength—responsible for carrying the weight of the world. These days, I'm taking notes from the butterfly, embracing the cycles of nature and transformation, allowing myself to more often dissolve into goop so I can emerge more beautifully and ready to fly again.

—Elyse Burden is the cofounder of Real World Scholars.

Laura: This story invites us to interrogate how the systems and norms we hold perpetuate the myth of our own failures and ultimately what it truly means to be honest about when we need help.

Stories like this inspire educators, parents, or coaches to dig deep and get real with ourselves by asking questions like:

- How did the system or structure we created or perpetuate contribute to failure?
- By whose standards, norms, or cultural values do you define failure?
- How are the lessons and practices setting young people on the path toward failure and potentially exacerbating inequalities?

Ron: I'd like to also invite our readers to think about this story, their own stories, and their own students' stories about honesty that might lead to new levels of awareness, new levels of practices, and create spaces where students and educators alike feel they can be honest and vulnerable. Within this story there are so many different levels connected to failure.

Obviously the story is about personal honesty, but the story shows us how failure is connected to both social and systems failure, which is grounded in a monolithic view of success and failure. When we use the pedagogy of sameness or fail to see race or our own biases, we just make assumptions about what it means to be successful. We need to disrupt what it means for our students to be successful.

I find it somewhat ironic that schools are places where learning is supposed to be happening, but in order to be seen as a successful learner you already have to know how to do everything. You already have to know the content and you have to know how to function socially and be savvy in navigating all the social challenges of a school, knowing how to fit in, and how to be a successful student. Educational leaders are expected to always know what to do to be successful even when facing new situations that are highly chaotic and uncertain.

So, it's really interesting that schools, which are supposedly places where we learn, feel like places where one has to be already fully competent in order to be successful. This story provokes us to ask:

- How can we examine the systems and inherited practices in which we work and disrupt them and make school a space where it's okay to be learning?
- How can we set back and ask for help and view those setbacks not as failures, but as signs of learning?
- How can we use this story or our own stories in our conversations with colleagues, staff, or community as a starting point to launch us into those conversations about how to be honest with ourselves, with others, and with the systems we work in to better support our own and others' learning from setbacks?

Chapter Ten

Humility

Cynthia Zhou: Original artwork
produced for this book

*We work, because we care. We care deeply about each other and about
our community, and that is always a lesson that needs repeating.*

—Kami Thordarson

Laura: One of the things that I love about the upcoming story is that the
author writes about designing something new that pushes on her own
capacities as an educator and leader. One of the unique parts of failure is
that it really pushes on our own learning edges and requires us to be really
humble about where we are in our learning processes and where our edges
for growth truly are as human beings.

Failure reminds us to be humble.

The author of the next story is a successful principal and teacher who
has written her own book on design and yet she is once again feeling
humbled during a staggering moment in education. Failures can be humbling because they challenge what we think we're really good at.

These humbling moments bring us back to the core of why we do what we do. They shine the light on what we think we can do and what we are not quite capable of yet. Humility can feel like egg on the face. It makes you think you did this awful thing, and you want to walk away with your tail between your legs.

And at the same time, the ability to be humble with our learning mistakes is an invitation to empathy. Humility is an invitation into curiosity. It is an invitation to connect more deeply with others. The humility we feel when we fail can renew our empathy for others. It invites us to be more empathetic and encourages us to listen more to the needs of others.

Ron: Design and planning are something that all humans do, and it's what educators and educational leaders do. We go into a design process or plan with some intention and assumptions, but failure highlights that even best intentions are received sometimes the opposite way that was intended.

In the next story the author used empathy and tried to be inclusive, and still there was a person who felt left out and alienated.

As educators, humility reminds us that we don't necessarily know what's best for the folks we're designing for. We must hold ourselves accountable to be humble, to check our assumptions, and to constantly check to see how our best intentions and actions are received.

Laura: That's right, Ron. Asking ourselves to think about how our work is going to impact someone is an important aspect to understanding failure but also understanding ourselves.

The story also highlights the paradox of humility in leadership. Traditional leadership models in education perpetuate the idea that a good or strong leader can manage it all. Principals are expected to manage the budget, staffing needs, instructional models, and more without the assistance of others.

These types of leadership suggest that individualism is a good tenet of leadership. But when we fail as leaders, perhaps it is because we did not ask for help. This tenet of individualism leads to isolation and sometimes results in moments of failure.

Humility, however, is grounded in the idea that I don't have the answers and I am vulnerable and brave enough to admit my shortcomings.

If we want to encourage our young people to take beautiful risks, we need to abandon the idea that failure is overcome through individual action.

One of the barriers to overcoming failure is having the humility to admit you need help, which means having enough humility to invite others into your world. How can we invite others into our moments of failure, not solve or find the solution but to serve as guides in rediscovering our own humility?

HUMILITY: MY FAVORITE FAILURE

By Kami Thordarson

I have been working in education for over twenty years now and have journeyed through the classroom as a teacher and through the school district office as a coach, principal, and director. Each experience has taught me so many new things, both about myself and what I want for our children regarding education.

Through the years I have taken a deep dive into design thinking, learning how to build mindsets and practices that create new opportunities and push our current educational practices into new pathways. My current role is as a principal and school designer for a growing preschool through eighth grade school out in California.

Here, we try to ground ourselves and our students in empathy. The year 2020 has brought many challenges and, as our school was only in its second year, every change has rocked our boat. I will say, however, that because we continue to value adaptability and we make caring a priority, our boat can rock fairly vigorously and we still manage to keep our footing.

Failure is a part of what we do and we value the learning that comes from the risk. I was recently reminded of that this spring.

The recent pandemic had sent all of us home, working diligently to keep students learning through technology. That alone came with a lot of new experiences and quick pivots as we moved through the learning curve. I was creating our end-of-the-year professional development experience, which needed to be two days long, all online. I decided that we needed a face-to-face moment as we had people leaving our staff and felt as though the personal community piece was missing.

I surveyed our staff to see who would be comfortable with coming onto campus, all safety protocols in place, and discovered that there was a large majority who were craving the same experience. We missed each other! We needed a moment, even if six feet apart, to connect and share. We did have a small group that was still uncomfortable coming back, and my challenge would be to find a way to meet both of the groups' needs. So, I got to work designing the two days of learning experiences.

The first day was built on different breakouts and working to involve everyone in meaningful conversations as much as possible. We built in screen breaks and found ways to meaningfully document and record our conversations. We had so much to reflect on and so much learning that we needed to sort through.

The second day was designed on campus, with some activities that might simulate how we would need to interact with students when school returned with the many new pandemic protocols. I thought of some ways for our staff that was off-site to "zoom" in and participate in a limited fashion. Here is where my failure came in.

At the end of our second day, I called to check in on those that had not been able to participate on campus. The first teacher I called cried. She was so distraught and disappointed with the experience. She felt completely left out and unable to participate. She felt abandoned. Here I was, continually waving the empathy flag, and I totally missed the mark in designing this experience.

When I asked her what we could have done so she felt included, she was able to come up with several great ideas that had never entered my head. And that was my biggest mistake. I was so wrapped up in creating these moments that I forgot who I was creating them for. Another mistake, thinking that "I" had to do all of the designing. I left my team, especially those that needed something different, out of the conversation.

We discuss empathy and ways to communicate with others in many of our conversations, both in how we interact and work with each other and how we educate our children. It's a grounding practice in this school. A teacher crying because they felt uncared for was an opportunity for me to practice humility and a lot of mindful listening. It also reminded me that there's a reason why we design to the edges.

In that rush to create this amazing end-of-year experience, I forgot to invite others to pick up a hammer. The reason our school is working and moving with change is that we are all contributing to the design and invested in the same blueprint. We work, because we care. We care deeply about each other and about our community and that is always a lesson that needs repeating.

—Kami Thordarson is principal and school designer at Campbell School of Innovation, Campbell, California.

Ron: I think it's sometimes difficult for leaders or people in leadership positions or positions of power to have the vulnerability or humility highlighted in this story. But setbacks remind us that we need to be humble in our expertise or experience. We have to examine our own confidence or assuredness in relation to others.

We also need to ask for help. Often people can get wrapped up in their experiences and expertise and feel like they are the one that's supposed to have the answers. Successful leaders are humble. They are vulnerable, they ask for help, they check in with others. They don't try to be isolated, and that is the path to learning and success.

Being overly confident and lacking humility seems to be the path to getting stuck and doing damage.

Sharing stories of favorite failures, being willing to talk about them is an exercise in humility, and it's also a way to signal that you are designing with people, not for them. Sharing stories is a way to learn from and support the learning of others. This story, and the concept of humility in relation to failure, invites us to reflect on questions like:

- How can we maintain and be reminded of our own humility and vulnerability while we are designing, doing, and reflecting on our processes?
- How can our own humility help us stay connected and not isolated in our work?

Laura: The topic of humility also reminds me about what is at stake if we don't see humility as the pivotal tool toward success. We have a lot of big sticky problems facing education. Between racial inequality, social justice, emerging technologies, and a rapidly changing job market that may not promise economic stability, it seems that our ability to be humble may be our most valuable asset in solving these problems.

A humble approach assumes we don't have the right answer yet and we need others.

As we consider the complexity of humility I am struck by the following questions:

- How can I cultivate the strength and humility to ask for help?
- How can we see our humility as the powerful tool for our own success and growth and not a reflection of failures?
- How might we practice humility daily in our conversations with others so we can truly hear and see their lived experiences?

Sharing this story and others in this book is an invitation to practice humility with the people around you. When we read and understand the facets of failure, we build empathy with others, which in turn broadens our perspective and worldview, making us capable of seeing the diverseness of solutions that are possible. Practicing humility is a lever for innovation, it's a lever for equity, it's a lever for really solving big problems.

Epilogue

For me, and, I am sure, for most of you, to be human is to be always in the process of becoming, to be in quest of openings, of possibilities. Always.

—Maxine Green

As we noted in the introduction, a key goal of this book is to start the process of learning from failure by listening to and sharing stories of favorite failures with others. The stories in this book show us that it is a beautiful risk to share favorite failures with others. We therefore hope you have learned from these stories and have been inspired to start sharing them and your own stories with others. Doing so is a bold, creative action.

These stories also unearth how the sharing of sometimes intensely personal experiences with others can take something that might have felt shameful to retell and transform it into a redemptive learning experience for everyone involved.

In this brief epilogue, we close with a brief discussion of four takeaways that we have from reading all these stories and working on this project.

FOUR TAKEAWAYS

There are at least four overarching takeaways that we would like to share from this book. Those four takeaways include: (1) importance of reckoning with failure; (2) failure feels isolating but is socially experienced;

(3) failure is an opportunity; and (4) failure and success are not binary. We briefly discuss each of these in turn.

We need to reckon with failure

This book serves an opportunity for all of us to reckon with failure and to really digest the vulnerable pieces of failure. In each story, we saw ourselves. While the moments of one's own lives were radically different, the emotion, the gut-wrenching moment of being frozen in front of others were very relatable. The shame we have felt when we let other people down or disappointment we felt when something we had designed, planned, and had high expectations for fell flat or worse unintentionally hurt someone else—all of these stories can evoke empathy and memories of past experiences.

In reading these stories, it is no wonder that we don't like to talk about failure! Many of us are afraid to admit our failures. We might feel disappointed in ourselves for failing to overcome the failure. In a world in which failure is only celebrated when you've had success, how do we create space in our classrooms and our lives for failure itself?

How can we reckon with the emotions we felt, the impact it had on our next steps, and how it created a lasting imprint that is now forever stitched on our memories?

These stories give us the power to reckon with our truths and our own stories about failure. Our ultimate hope, however, is that these stories are taken a step further and shared with young people to help them anticipate, navigate, and be willing to share their own stories of learning from setbacks. As educators we've often said, "try—you'll be okay, you might fail but you will be okay."

On the surface and in the moment that feels right but in reading these stories, those suggestions are often superficial because they don't address the immediate, emotional pain of setbacks or the long-term impact that those moments can have on us. In reflection on the power of sharing stories of failure, we have started to recognize that doing so can change how we see ourselves, how we approach the world, and how we see others. We hope that the stories in this book inspire you and others to explore the fabric of failure, allowing you to not only learn from setbacks but also open the conversation up with others about failure, learning, and growth.

Failure Is Felt Individually but Experienced Together

The second takeaway we have from these stories is that reckoning with failure provides us with a chance to shift away from viewing failure as an isolated individual act and toward an opportunity to see failure as a social act of vulnerability and service.

These stories help us to uncover the responsibility we have to each other in moments of failure.

Although the stories we've collected for this book may differ from your own experiences and stories, we hope you can recognize, empathize, and learn from the emotions and insights that they represent. If we can relate to some features of these stories, then what is our responsibility to each other, to young people when they are in the midst of failure? Failures are often experienced by individuals but are felt collectively. What is the responsibility of a community to hold space for others through moments of crisis, failure, and setbacks?

How do we engage and support others in the moments when we see failure coming straight at us—those moments where we feel that uncomfortable knocking in our belly; where we feel the moment where we are about to fall? How do we literally extend a physical and supportive hand to each other?

These stories also displace the way failure is usually located. Sometimes failure is part of the environment around us. Failure is often experienced as an isolating experience. Suddenly, you become immediately outside of everything else that's happening.

People often feel alone and alienated when they encounter failures and setbacks. In public failures, we feel spotlighted and even pushed outside of the community. Our sense of belonging feels shattered. These stories teach us that failure is a shared experience. It doesn't belong to just the one person that's experiencing it. It is a shared event. In this way failures can help establish an autonomy supportive (rather than controlling) classroom environment (Reeve, 2009), which welcomes opportunities to learn and grow from our own and others' setbacks.

We feel that this is an important message for parents, teachers, and coaches who are trying to support young people through the inevitable failures and setbacks that they're going to experience. Specifically, when we work together to establish an emotionally and psychologically supportive learning environment (Ryan & Deci, 2000), we can help young people re-establish their sense of belonging as well as be supported in developing their sense of competence and even autonomy when they encounter setbacks.

We hope these stories and dialogues in this book, as well as your own conversations with colleagues and young people, will help you in antici-pating the moments of setback students might experience and be better prepared to establish and provide just-in time supports, structures, and activities to remind them that they are not alone, that failure is part of the human experience and an integral part of learning.

Failure is an opportunity

The third insight that we had when reading and discussing these stories was the idea that seeing failure as a communal act also gives us an opportunity to interrogate the cultural, racial, and societal norms and structures in play during moments of failure. This raised questions for us about the features of learning environments that might be sending or reinforcing the messages that make young people feel like failures when they encounter setbacks, rather than viewing setbacks as opportunities to learn and grow from failures.

This raises multiple questions to reflect on in any learning environment, such as: Who has the privilege to experience failure as a learning oppor-tunity (rather than an indictment of the self)? What are the conditions or cultural expectations around failure? Who or what is deemed a failure? Who decides what is an act of failure versus an act of creative divergence?

How might discussing stories of failure provide an opportunity to explore how a particular behavior, norm, or act reveals cultural, racial, or societal norms? How do we use these stories of failure as insights for interrogating the sometimes-hidden and problematic curricular norms and expectations on which our schools are built?

Failure is often seen as a stepping-stone in pursuit of success. And yet for many of our most marginalized students, failure is another example of a system that systematically oppressed their identity, positionality, and culture.

Failure to "meet expectations" in expected and predetermined ways can be a constant reminder that difference is not welcomed or even that the rules governing how young people are expected to perform in school can result in feeling like there is only one, narrow and limited path to learning and success.

Failure to adhere to norms and expectations, often white dominant norms and expectations, can serve as a constant reminder that different ways of knowing and being are not welcomed. Stories of favorite failures can raise the questions, such as who has the privilege to fail and how might educators disrupt problematic systems, norms, and practices that frame people as failures rather than view moments of failures as opportunities for engaging with difference and growing from the insights, reflections, and vulnerability that come from those experiences.

These stories also raise the question around the stakes surrounding failure. What is perceived as potentially low stakes for one person, such as standing up in front of a group of peers, feels different for other people based on their race, language, or gender. As shown in one story, the risk of failing in your first public presentation in a language different from your native language feels like high-risk failure. For others, a high risk may feel like failing to fit into the community you thought you were invited to.

Uncovering these failures and discussing them as a community can help us see the barriers to learning and success. We start to see how the fabric of failure is connected to and often reinforces inequality. We begin to see that features of the systems, like standardized tests and fixed curricula, are devoid of pluralistic perspectives and can thereby perpetuate structural and systemic inequalities.

If we want *all young* people to succeed in learning and life, we need to honestly examine our own and other people's failures as opportunities to reveal and address problematic features of the systems in which we work.

How can we dedicate ourselves to understanding the failures that surround learning not just from an analytical or academic perspective, but from the perspective of what it feels like to fail? If young people have experienced educational systems that do not honor their identity, perspective, or race—where success has been continuously viewed through the dominant narrative—then failure might feel inevitable.

Given the high-stakes risk of failing in a system that does not honor you, it is no wonder if young people who experience that marginalization might be disengaged in school. How might we draw on stories in this book to help examine when features of the system are really failing and not the person who is experiencing that failure?

The stories in this book prompt all of us who work within and design for educational institutions and designers to examine who or what is failing a young person to succeed. We hope these stories will help us all to engage in the work necessary to examine, identify, and address behaviors and norms that are failing our young people by making success feel like it is unattainable and instead move toward establishing educational environments of continual learning and support when we are experiencing sometimes painful setbacks and failures.

Failure and Success Are Not Binary

The fourth insight that we have drawn from these stories is that they can help us recognize how failure is an integral part of the learning process. Failure and setbacks cannot really be separated from learning and success.

Many of us are afraid to admit our failures. We might feel embarrassed. We might feel disappointed. One reason why we might feel this way is because we often only celebrate failure after someone has experienced success. It is easy to discuss failures from the vantage point of success. You can look back on those failures with a smile, stand up and say, "I had 1,200 failures but now my project succeeded."

When we only discuss and share failures after success, we artificially distance the two from each other. We are either experiencing failure or success. We stay in failure until we can step into success. This false dichotomy separating success and failure is prevalent in our experiences in and out of school.

We're taught to see the grade of an "A" as success and the grade of an "F" as failure. How can we see the successes in the moments of failure and even the failures in our moments of success? How might sharing stories of favorite failures help us look at, really look, at moments of success and failure as always connected? How might doing so uncover all the emotions, learning, and insights that these experiences reveal about ourselves, our communities, culture and the systems we live within? Can we begin to see the learning in the in-between space of success and failure?

In this book, we've read and discussed stories of failure from people who were willing to take the risk of sharing them. We've sat with these stories and discussed them in an attempt to see how failure is not just one moment or one set of emotions but much more complex assemblages of experiences and emotions that can help us approach our work with young people with more humility and better support them in who they are trying to become.

References

Aoki, T. T. (2004). Spinning inspirited images. In W. F. Pinar & R. L. Irwin (Eds.), *Curriculum in a new key: The collected works of Ted T. Aoki* (pp. 413–425). Mahwah, NJ: Lawrence Erlbaum Associates.

Baert, P. (1991). Unintended consequences: A typology and examples. *International Sociology, 6*(2), 201–210. https://doi.org/10.1177/026858091006002006

Beghetto, R. A. (2022). Failure and creativity. To appear in J. A. Plucker (Ed.)., *Creativity and Innovation: Theory, Research, and Practice* (2nd Ed.)*.* Waco, TX: Prufrock Press.

Beghetto, R. A. (2021). My favorite failure: Using digital technology to facilitate creative learning and reconceptualize failure. *Tech Trends.* https://doi .org/10.1007/s11528-021-00607-7

Beghetto, R. A. (2019). *Beautiful risks: Having the courage to teach and learn creatively.* New York: Rowman & Littlefield.

Beghetto, R. A. (2018). Taking beautiful risks in education. *Educational Leadership, 76*(4), 18–24.

Beghetto, R. A. (2017). Creative openings in the social interactions of teaching. *Creativity: Theories-Research-Applications, 3,* 261–273.

Beghetto, R. A. (2013). *Killing ideas softly? The promise and perils of creativity in the classroom.* Charlotte, NC: Information Age Publishing.

Beghetto, R. A., & Dilley, A. E. (2016). Creative aspirations or pipe dreams? Toward understanding creative mortification in children and adolescents. *New Directions for Child and Adolescent Development, 151,* 85–95.

Berns, G. (2010). *Iconoclast. A neuroscientist reveals how to think differently.* Boston: Harvard Business School Publishing.

Brown. B. (2020). *The gifts of imperfection.* New York: Random House.

Bruner, J. (1991). The narrative construction of reality. *Critical Inquiry, 18,* 1–21.

Byrnes, J. P. (2011). *The nature and development of decision-making: A self-regulation model.* New York: Psychology Press.

Dow, S. P., Glassco, A., Kass, J., Schwarz, M., Schwartz, D. L., and Klemmer, S. R. 2010. Parallel prototyping leads to better design results, more divergence, and increased self-efficacy. ACM Trans. Comput.-Hum. Interact. 17, 4, Article 18 (December 2010), 24 pages. doi.acm.org/10.1145/1879831.1879836

Dweck, C. (2007). *Mindset: The new psychology of success*. New York: Ballantine Books.

Escobar, A. (2018). *Designs for the pluriverse: Radical interdependence, autonomy, and the making of worlds*. Durham, NC: Duke University Press.

Fried, R. L. (2005). *The game of school: Why we all play it, how it hurts kids, and what it will take to change it*. San Francisco: Jossey-Bass.

Gay, G. (2002). Preparing for culturally responsive teaching. *Journal of Teacher Education, 53*, 106–116.

Glăveanu, V. P. (2020). *Wonder: The extraordinary power of an ordinary experience*. London: Bloomsbury.

Glăveanu, V. P., & Beghetto, R. A. (2020). Creative experience: A non-standard definition of creativity. *Creativity Research Journal, 33*, 75–80.

Grant, A., & Coyle, D. (2018). The process of building trust works in the opposite way that you think it does. https://work.qz.com/1241911/ daniel-coyle-author -of-the-the-culture-code-says-building-trustworks-in-the-opposite-way-you -think-it-does/?mc_cid= 015ae0d31b&mc_eid=427e2dccd0

Hiebert, J., & Grouws, D. (2007). The effects of classroom mathematics teaching on students' learning. In F. K. Lester Jr. (Ed.), *Second handbook of research on mathematics teaching and learning* (pp. 371–404). Charlotte, NC: Information Age Publishing.

Hoffmann, J. D., Ivcevic, Z., & Maliakkal, N. (2020). Emotions, creativity, and the arts: Evaluating a course for children. *Empirical Studies of the Arts*. https:// doi.org/10.1177/027623742090786

Kapur, M. (2008). *Productive failure. Cognition and Instruction, 26*, 379–424. https://doi.org/10.1080/07370000802212669

Kapur, M. (2016). Examining productive failure, productive success, unproductive failure, and unproductive success in learning. *Educational Psychologist, 51*(2), 289–299. https://doi.org/10.1080/ 00461520.2016.1155457

Lambert, J., & Hessler, H. B. (2018). *Digital storytelling: Capturing lives, creating community* (5th Ed., revised and updated). New York: Routledge, Taylor & Francis Group.

Manalo, E., & Kapur, M. (2018). The role of failure in promoting thinking skills and creativity: New findings and insights about how failure can be beneficial for learning. *Thinking Skills and Creativity, 30*, 1–6. https://doi.org/10.1016/j .tsc.2018.06.001

McBain, L. J., & Solomon L. K. *Educator as futurist: Moving beyond "preparing for the future" to "shaping the future."* Medium. October 5, 2020. https://medium.com/stanford-d-school/educator-as-futurist-moving-beyond-preparing-for-the-future-to-shaping-the-future-56d8b4346364

Reeve, J. (2009). Why teachers adopt a controlling motivating style toward students and how they can become more autonomy supportive. *Educational Psychologist, 44*, 159–175.

Rosiek, J., & Beghetto, R. A. (2009). Emotional scaffolding: The emotional and imaginative dimensions of teaching and learning. In P. A. Schutz & M. Zembylas (Eds.), *Advances in teacher emotion research* (pp. 175–194). Springer US. https://doi.org/10.1007/978- 1-4419-0564-2_9

Ryan, R. M., & Deci, E. L. (2000). Intrinsic and extrinsic motivations: Classic definitions and new directions. *Contemporary Educational Psychology, 25*, 54–67.

Scheff, T. J. (2003). Shame in self and society. *Symbolic Interaction, 26*, 239–262. doi:10.1525/si.2003.26.2.239

Snowden, D. J., & Boone, M. E. (2007). A leader's framework for decision making. *Harvard Business Review, 85*, 68.

Stein Greenberg, S. (2021). *Creative acts for curious people: How to think, create, and lead in unconventional ways*. New York: Ten Speed Press.

Tracy, J. L., & Robins, R. W. (2004). Putting the self into self-conscious emotions: A theoretical model. *Psychological Inquiry, 15*(2), 103–125. https://doi.org/10.1207/s15327965pli1502_01

von Thienen, J., Meinel, M., & Corazza, G. E. (2017). A short theory of failure. *Electronic Colloquium on Design Thinking Research, 17*, 1–5.

Whitney, D. K., & Trosten-Bloom, A. (2010). *The power of appreciative inquiry: A practical guide to positive change*. San Francisco: Berrett-Koehler Publishers.

Wood, D., Bruner, J., & Ross, G. (1976). The role of tutoring in problem solving. *Journal of Child Psychology and Psychiatry, 17*, 89–100.

About the Authors

Ronald A. Beghetto, PhD (Ronald.Beghetto@asu.edu), is an internationally recognized expert on creative thought and action in educational settings. He holds the Pinnacle West Presidential Chair and serves as a professor in the Mary Lou Fulton Teachers College at Arizona State University. Ron is the editor for the *Journal of Creative Behavior* and for *Review of Research in Education*, as well as series editor for *Creative Theory and Action in Education*, and he has served as a creativity advisor for LEGO Foundation and the Cartoon Network. He is also a Fellow of the American Psychological Association, the Society for the Psychology of Aesthetics, Creativity and the Arts (Div. 10, APA), and the International Society for the Study of Creativity and Innovation (ISSCI). More information about Ron can be found at www.ronaldbeghetto.com.

Laura McBain (she/her) (@laura_mcbain) is a designer, an educator, and the codirector of the K–12 lab at the Stanford d.school. As a human-centered designer, her work focuses on understanding the ecosystem of education and finding meaningful opportunities to advance racial and social justice. Prior to the d.school, Laura worked for 15 years at High Tech High, serving as the director of External Relations, principal of two school sites, and a founding teacher. She has taught middle and high school students in both charter and comprehensive schools. Laura has a bachelor's degree from Miami University-Oxford, Ohio, and a masters from the Harvard Graduate School of Education.